Ervin (Earl) Cobb and Charlotte D. ⸻

PRAISE FOR THEIR WORK

"There is nothing better than a good story. Utilizing very relevant stories that you can easily identify with tied to the highly actionable Skinny Principles makes for a great formula. A very useful and timely book for all professionals looking to advance their leadership skills."
— **Barbara Cooper, CIO Toyota North America – Retired**

"Charlotte and Earl are leaders and can teach leadership; a rare combination. The Smart Leader should hold a prominent place in your professional library."
— **Jim Grigsby, President/CEO Jim Grigsby Consulting**

"Master Teachers is my description of these authors. The Smart Leader is a must read for all leaders; especially for generations of future leaders."
— **Selma C. Dean, ED.D. , Pastoral and Community Counselor, Educator, Inspirational Speaker**

"An excellent read! Concise and to the point"
— **Rhonda Culver, Owner/ Broker, Culver Realty**

"Written from practical experience and success. An inspiration!"
— **Robert Bunnett, Chief Operating Officer, LSI**

"Earl Cobb has done it again with his new book. Earl is that rarest of authors. He writes with the power of someone who has been there."
— **Doug Russell, Marketing Director, SmartPro Financial**

"Mr. Cobb has captured the pure essence of Leadership in this work. His broad-based experience guides his insight in every topical area."
— **Albert L. McHenry, Ph.D., Emeritus Faculty, Arizona State University**

Ervin (Earl) Cobb and Charlotte D. Grant-Cobb, PhD
PRAISE FOR THEIR WORK

"As major transitions in the world are transpiring, leadership requires a broader and deeper understanding of today's organizations and the individuals that lead them. The SMART Leader and the "Skinny" Principles proffers that leaders are expected to act and think differently, not just to survive, but to thrive in this changing organizational landscape."

"For some, these changes are exciting, exhilarating, and long overdue. But for many in the organizational hierarchy, the breadth of new challenges appears enormous. In this book, storytelling is used as a medium which allows the reader to engage and see themselves in the story. Through this journey, they build confidence in attitude, actions, and skills to succeed."

— **Rufus Glasper, Ph.D., President and CEO, League for Innovation, Chancellor Emeritus, Maricopa Community Colleges**

"Busy leaders need practical guidance and an easy-to-follow format which is what this book provides. The authors have culled their years of experience and in a story format. By doing so, they have provided a path for leaders to follow. I hope others may benefit from their expertise and apply the "Skinny" Principles to their respective paths. Kudos!"

— **Dr. G. Mick Smith, Executive Regional Director, Challenger School Foundation**

"I have a shelf full of leadership books. With rare exceptions, those books don't really help anyone lead in the real world. But, Earl and Charlotte's new book, *The SMART Leader*, sure does. If you only get one book on leadership this year, make it this one. Simple and insightful guidelines and stories that stick. You can't beat it."

—**Doug Russell, Financial Coach and Author of** *Every-Day Living: Memories of a Family from Blaine, North Carolina.*

Ervin (Earl) Cobb and Charlotte D. Grant-Cobb, PhD
PRAISE FOR THEIR WORK

"Mr. Cobb has been meticulously working on advancing what is known in the realm of Leadership Development. He is a proven author of several books, a well-known speaker, a leader, and has a genius approach to leadership development. The information that he provides in his latest body of work is "textbook worthy" and I highly recommend all colleges/universities/companies adopt this body of work to teach Leadership Development."

— Jonathan Hebert, M. Eng, PMP, Ph.D., Program Manager/Raytheon, Owner/Randy Brevard Holdings

"The Cobbs have written a leadership book that is easy to read with practical, apply it right now, techniques. This book is chock full of tips, techniques, and best practices in leadership that will be of value to new leaders of any generation. Their "Skinny" Principles, shared in each chapter, will undoubtedly be earmarked and highlighted by readers and referred to regularly. This book is a MUST READ for new leaders. Plus, leaders who have been in their role for a while will likely also find a nugget or two to take away and apply."

— Gina Abudi, MBA, President, Abudi Consulting Group, LLC, Author of *Implementing Positive Organizational Change: A Strategic Project Management Approach*, J Ross Publishing, 2017

"The book is EXCEPTIONAL & definitely a must read!!!! The principles are helping me transition from "managing" my team at my organization to "leading" my team."

— Glori Allen, BlueCross BlueShield of South Carolina Information Systems Training Manager.

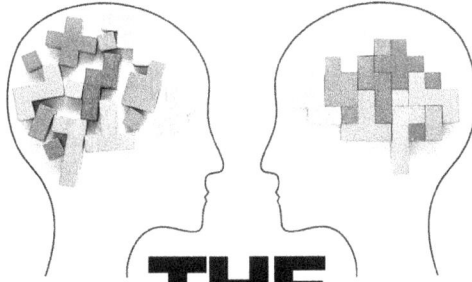

THE
SMART
LEADER
AND THE "SKINNY" PRINCIPLES

We dedicate this book to you, the reader. Your willingness to take the time to read this book and learn how the "Skinny" Principles can make a difference in your leadership success inspires us. It is our hope that you make the commitment to deploy what you have gained and reap the benefits of becoming a SMART Leader.

Published by RICHER Press
An Imprint of Richer Life, LLC
5710 Ogeechee Road #200-175
Savannah, Georgia 31405
www.richerlifellc.com

Cover Design: RICHER Media USA

Volume book discounts are available for groups, companies and organizations. Contact the publisher for information and order instructions.

Library of Congress Cataloging-in-Publications Data

THE SMART LEADER AND THE SKINNY PRINCIPLES
How to Lead and Win within Any Organization

Ervin (Earl) Cobb and Charlotte D. Grant-Cobb, PhD
p.   cm.

1. Leadership   2. Management   3. Self-Improvement
(pbk : alk. Paper)

2019904585

ISBN-13: 978-1-7335693-0-9
ISBN-10: 1-7335693-0-8

PRINTED IN THE UNITED STATES OF AMERICA

September 19, 2019

SITUATIONAL NARRATIVES

	TITLE	PROTAGONIST
Chapter 1	No, My Dear. You Have A Leadership Dilemma	Marilynn Mason-Lee, MBA Manager (GS-14), Federal Government Agency
Chapter 2	I Thought They Really Knew Me	Mark Ashford, MBA, PMP Corporate Manager of Proje Management
Chapter 3	I Was Born To Do This	CeCe Lane, PhD, Art Teach Small Business Owner
Chapter 4	I Simply Played The Cards I Was Dealt	Sara Hornbill, CEO, Walbas International, Multi-Nationa Specialty Products Company
Chapter 5	An Astonishing Lack Of Leadership Presence	Anthony Jerome McAdoo 30-year Corporate Retiree an Leadership Development Consultant
Chapter 6	I Didn't Expect This	Rebecca Bushman, MBA Regional Vice President, Roland Pharmaceuticals
Chapter 7	Now, It Makes Sense	Candace Campbell, BA, MA Chief of Police, City of Phoenix
Chapter 8	The Trees Got Me	Frances Rodriquez, Lead Supervisor, Miracle Mile Aerospace
Chapter 9	I Only Needed To Be Like Mike	Charlie Yang, President and CEO, The Better Way Foundation
Chapter 10	I Should Have Known	Julie Juliet, MSEE, PhD President and CEO, Robote Inc.

CONTENTS

NOTE FROM THE AUTHORS

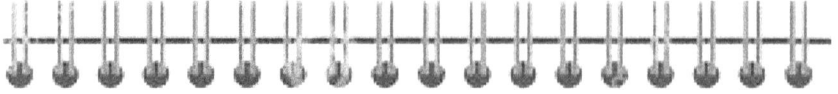

A few years ago, we first had the opportunity to integrate the power of *Narrative Enhanced Leadership Development* or NELD into our literary work. Based on the awesome feedback from our readership, we have witnessed the impact that NELD can have on increasing reader focus, comprehension and enjoyment.

NELD is a learning and knowledge retention technique, which activates the brain of readers or listeners by turning stories and situational narratives into their own experiences.

According to Gerry Beamish, a UK consultant who researches the value of storytelling in accelerating learning, *"A story is the only way to activate parts in the brain so that a listener turns the story into their own ideas and experiences."*

Therefore, NELD works because, as humans, we are all wired to allow good stories to help us to walk in someone else's shoes and actually gain the experience.

The SMART Leader and the "Skinny" Principles utilizes the NELD knowledge retention technique. You will find that each chapter is introduced by a compelling and suspenseful *situational narrative*. Each narrative is written to "cut to the chase" and help you to instantly benefit from the suggestions and guidance provided in the discussion of each *"Skinny" Principle*.

So, go ahead. Allow your brain to be activated and internalize the lessons learned by the protagonist in each narrative.

By combining the knowledge of their experiences with a good grasp of all ten *"Skinny" Principles*, you will be on your way to becoming a SMART Leader.

INTRODUCTION

LEADING AND WINNING

As **we all know**, while walking the tight rope of all professional endeavors, everything seems to consistently center around these four questions, *"What"*, *"Why"*, *"How"* and *"When"*.

What should I do? Why should I do it? How should I do it? When is the best and most effective time to do it?

Yes. Most of this book is about something we call the *"Skinny" Principles* and the positive impact these straightforward yet meaty perceptions and leadership strengthening actions can have in the professional and personal lives of everyone involved in leading or being led within an organization.

However, the overarching objective of this book is to provide you with a new and contemporary guide that can help you, as the leader, and your organization accomplish your two most important responsibilities. The first is your responsibility to get the most out of the resources being invested to achieve the expected results. The second is doing it in a way that *failure is not an option*. In other words, making sure that you are always in the position where you and your organization have a high probability of *leading* and *winning*.

Therefore, we decided that the best way to begin the introduction of *The Smart Leader and the "Skinny" Principles* is with a brief discussion of the "What", "Why", "How" and "When" that drives the powerful perspective associated with *leading* and *winning*.

The *"What"*, in a nutshell, is the fact and the reality that all organizations must both *lead* and *win* in order to justify their long-term existence. In our globally competitive world, whether your organization is for-profit, non-profit, civic or governmental, there is always someone or something competing for the resources that you have been given.

"Why" is keeping this perspective top of mind in your *leadership* role so important? It is important for a couple of key reasons:

1. Only strong, confident and effective *leadership* can deliver the environment, direction and impact required to get the most out of the resources invested in you and your organization; and

2. Winning is the only alternative to not failing.

"How" will or should this be accomplished?

Well, of course, all pertinent members of the organization, from the top to the bottom, have a role in accomplishing the tasks required to achieve the organization's goals. However, the difference between *winning* and *failing* heavily depends on the presence of strong, confident and effective *leadership* at the top.

As the organization's leader, you play a highly visible and essential role. The leadership you provide must include the operative use of the appropriate management skills as well as the energy, influence, inspiration and passion required to win and not fail. The proper balance between *management acumen* and *leadership skills* is extremely vital to *winning* and achieving the desired results.

According to Warren Bennis, scholar, organizational consultant and widely regarded pioneer of the contemporary field of leadership studies, *"Failing organizations are usually over-managed and under-led."*

Therefore, you and your organization will succeed – meet your expectations and not fail – largely because of your ability to *"not just do things right"* but to also *"do the right things"* necessary to confidently and consistently *manage, lead* and *win*.

This brings us to the *"When"*.

When is the best and most effective time for you, as the leader, to possess the leadership skills and insights needed to ensure victory? Certainly, the best time is prior to accepting the leadership role. The second-best time is *right now*.

We believe that by deciding to take the time now to absorb the *"Skinny" Principles* and to acquire what it takes to become a SMART Leader, you are certainly off to a great start.

However, only a true commitment to mastering these *Principles* and fully integrating them into your daily leadership approach can place you and your organization in the enviable position of always *leading* and *winning*.

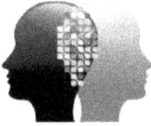

WHAT OTHERS ARE THINKING

"Leadership is not about a title or a designation. It's about impact, influence and inspiration. Impact involves getting results, influence is about spreading the passion you have for your work, and you have to inspire team-mates and customers." — Robin S. Sharma

Robin S. Sharma

Robin Sharma is a Canadian writer known for his *"The Monk Who Sold His Ferrari"* book series. He is one of the world's premier speakers on Leadership and Personal Mastery, recently named one of the World's Top Leadership Gurus.

LEADERSHIP AND ORGANIZATIONAL SUCCESS

All **organizations regardless** of the type or size have five *foundational components* in common.

The first four are *tangible* components. They are material, perceptible and substantial in the definition of an organization. The fifth component is unique in that it is at all times comprised of both *tangible* and *intangible* qualities.

The first four foundational components are *Purpose*, *People*, *Processes* and *Politics*.

The presence, influence and impact of these components in organizational success or failure are easily observed and quickly understood by anyone familiar with organizational performance and organizational culture. Without a meaningful *purpose*, the right *people*, the appropriate *processes* and adequate control of internal and external *politics*, any organization will fail to achieve its mission and soon fail to exist.

The fifth and arguably the most important component is much more complex in nature and utilizes both *tangible* and *intangible* qualities or *talents* in a strategic and complementary manner.

The fifth component is, of course, YOU, the person selected or regarded as the leader of the organization and the owner of the leadership responsibilities that come with the job.

As the leader, your *tangible* qualities are most transparent when you perform the roles that are expected of you on a daily basis. These roles are routinely *learned* in the classroom, *actualized* through training and *perfected* with experience.

The *tangible* qualities of you the *Leader* and you the *Manager* are undistinguishable – alias, the planner, the organizer, the staffer, the director, and the controller.

However, your *intangible* qualities are what distinguish you the *Leader* from you the *Manager*.

We view these leadership qualities as *intangible* because their transformative impact can't benefit the organization and its mission simply by a leader's physical presence. The power of these *intangible* qualities can only be released through a leader's actions, personality, personal influence and other human virtues.

Now, perfecting the art of strategically and systematically deploying these *intangible* leadership qualities does require numerous and diverse leadership opportunities and years of practice.

However, we believe that all good managers and supervisors can eliminate fundamental shortcomings and become a more *effective* leader in the near-term if they are willing to:

1. Take the time and make the effort to understand and master a few straightforward *truths* or *principles* that are fundamental to *leading* and *winning* within organizational structures; and

2. Commit to enhancing five specific personal qualities that set all *Leaders* apart from most *Managers*.

The specific qualities or *attributes* are present in most high achievers at all levels within most organizations. They are psychologically and intuitively inherent to being what we call **SMART** or **S**tudious, **M**asterful, **A**rticulate, **R**esourceful and **T**rustworthy.

In the next section of this Introduction, you will gain more insight into what it means to be a SMART Leader and the personal and professional value in mastering the perceptions and leadership-strengthening actions set forth in our discussion of the *"Skinny Principles"*.

The most important thing to remember, at this point, is that this book and its contents can only serve as a guide to how you can become a more effective leader within your organization.

The actual results and benefits you gain will be directly proportional to the time and the level of focused effort you invest in this *transformational* and *thought-provoking* self-improvement journey.

We have included throughout the book some *fundamental truths* and a few select quotes by individuals who are considered thought-leaders. We suggest that you keep the essence of these insights *top of mind* as your personal journey – *challenges, demands* and *reward*s.

- *Challenges* your comfort level.
- *Demands* the necessary changes in your thought process and leadership perspective.
- *Rewards* you with organizational influence, respect and leadership success.

We have also included within the book a few simple but effective tools you can use to take a *deeper dive* into understanding, mastering and benefiting from the *"Skinny" Principles*.

WHAT OTHERS ARE THINKING

"Leadership contains certain elements of good management, but it requires that you inspire, that you build durable trust. For an organization to be not just good but to win, leadership means evoking participation larger than the job description, commitment deeper than any job contract's wording." — Stanley A. McChrystal

Stanley A. McChrystal
Stanley McChrystal is a retired United States Army general best known for his command of Joint Special Operations Command in the mid-2000s.

THE SMART LEADER AND THE "SKINNY" PRINCIPLES

Principles are mostly accepted as fundamental beliefs, truths, concepts or values that serve as a good guide for behavior or evaluation.

The SMART Leader builds upon a carefully chosen collection of what we call *"Skinny" Principles.*

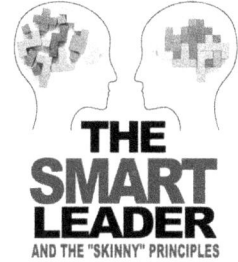

These *"Skinny" Principles* insightfully and candidly *cut to the chase* and simplify what must be done to address the hard-core realities embedded within the challenging art of successfully leading within 21st century organizational structures.

All of the *Principles* are closely connected to organizational success, intelligently leading others within organizations and what it takes for you to become a truly authentic, organizational leader. The concise, yet potent, *Principles* are deeply anchored in years of academic study and the real-world experiences of thousands of very successful and adequately equipped leaders within organizations of all types and sizes.

We believe that anyone can *lead* and *win* within any organization if they dedicate the time required to understand and to master these ten *"Skinny" Principles* and the straightforward leadership strengthening actions set forth in this book.

The *"Skinny" Truth* is that becoming a SMART Leader does not require extraordinary talents, advanced degrees or years of leadership experience. However, it does require you, as a leader, to always be **S**tudious, **M**asterful, **A**rticulate, **R**esourceful and **T**rustworthy — or **SMART**. We believe that these are the five personal attributes that set *Leaders* apart from *Managers.*

At the end of the book, you will find *The SMART Leader Archetype Overview,* which details the characteristics and leadership tendencies of each personal attribute.

In ten short chapters, you will be provided the *What, Why, How* and *When* associated with mastering the *"Skinny" Principles*.

Each chapter is introduced by a contemporary, compelling and suspenseful *situational narrative*. All of the narratives are written to help guide good managers supervisors to tackle the leadership challenges they are facing today or will face the future.

You will discover that the book's concise yet meaningful discussions construct both a contextual and convincing case for each of the ten "Skinny" Principles.

The SMART Leader is written to thoughtfully challenge anyone currently in a leadership role or aspire to move into a leadership position. The book's candid discussions and specific suggestions are structured to assist you in wisely taking the actions required to eliminate fundamental leadership shortcomings. By doing so, you will be rewarded with an increased level of performance and valuable organizational influence.

The goal is not for you to just become a more effective leader. It is for you and your organization to be in the position to always *lead* and *win*.

CHAPTER ONE

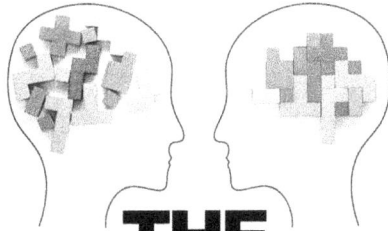

THE
SMART
LEADER
AND THE "SKINNY" PRINCIPLES

IT DOES MATTER

WHAT OTHERS ARE THINKING

"Effective leadership is the only competitive advantage that will endure. That's because leadership has two sides: what a person is (character) and what a person does (competence)."
— Stephen R. Covey

Stephen R. Covey

Stephen Covey is an American educator, author, businessperson and keynote speaker. His most popular book is *"The 7 Habits of Highly Effective People"*.

A Situational Narrative

NO, MY DEAR. YOU HAVE A LEADERSHIP DILEMMA

My name is Marilynn Renee Mason-Taylor. I have always been a focused, hardworking manager. I have both a BA and MBA.

However, I currently feel incredibly lonely, defeated and like a real loser. Here's why.

Over the past fifteen years, I have worked my way up the ranks of a major federal government Agency. Three years ago, I was promoted to the grade of GS-14. A year ago, I was selected over ten other candidates to lead the organization and new function within the same Agency.

Unlike any of the organizations I have managed in the past, more than eighty percent of my new team is under thirty-five years of age. Half of them work predominantly from home. Most of my team members are also new to this Agency and have a lot to learn about the operational processes and goals of the new function.

But, with my wealth of management experience at various levels within this Agency, I felt that I could teach them how the "old guys" do it and give them a "leg up" compared to their co-workers in other organizations. In addition, since I was at least 10 years older than most of them, I assumed that they would easily listen to me and follow my carefully worded directions.

When I accepted this position, the idea of creating and leading a new Agency organization and functional operation appeared to be a great opportunity. I was looking forward to reaching the enviable, GS-15 grade in short order.

Well, the past twelve months have been the worst period in my entire career. My health is failing. My manager has less time to spend with me. My co-workers are not as talkative when I am around them these days and I find it difficult to get up and come in to work. Over the last few weeks, I have been waking up concerned that I would soon be replaced or even dismissed, and my career would be in shambles.

Here is some of what has occurred since I took over the new organization and why I now feel so defeated.

- Three months into my new management role, I was drowning in internal meetings and conference calls involving almost every member of my team. There were so many calls and so many questions that I had to institute a policy that would limit our team meetings to one forty-five-minute gathering per week. All conference calls must now have to be approved, at least a week in advance. I was also forced to change my office "open door" policy from anytime to only two hours a day on Wednesdays and Fridays.

- Limiting the communications with and between my team members did have the effect of slowing down what I thought were unproductive meetings and calls. However, within a few months, more and more team members began to miss important deadlines. I found myself having to meet with each one of them individually to ensure that everyone knew what I expected. I used the time to let them know that I was not pleased with their job performance and I knew that they could do better. I also made sure they knew what I would not tolerate.

- Last fall, I was forced to cancel the annual Team Holiday Party. Through the grapevine, I found out that many of my team members were spending time with managers in other Agency organizations chatting and complaining about how my department's operational processes didn't allow them to make real time decisions that would reduce inefficiencies and complete more work in less time. Yet not even one of my team members bothered to bring any of these suggestions to my attention.

I feel that things really began to go downhill a few weeks ago. I learned that when I missed the first half a quarterly meeting with my co-workers and our Agency's top executives that much of that time was spent discussing how poorly my organization was functioning. Also, my peers shared that they were concerned about how my team is not working productively with the other teams within the Agency.

Last week, I accidentally ran into an old friend and mentor who I have known since graduate school. Over coffee, I shared with him my current management dilemma.

He sat quietly for a while and finally said, *"No, my dear. You have a leadership dilemma."* Then, he asked me three questions that I could not answer affirmatively, and that I will never forget:

1. *"When you accepted the position, did you consider what leadership skills you would need to successfully lead a new organization?"*

2. *"Have you had any training in what it takes and how to lead millennials?"*

3. *"It sounds like to me that your actions and thinking are those of a manager and not a leader. Are you aware of the difference between managing and leading?"*

I must admit that I did take a few courses in graduate school where we discussed leadership styles and common leadership traits.

However, I never took any of that stuff seriously.

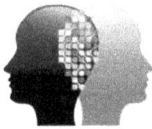

WHAT OTHERS ARE THINKING

"Effective leadership is putting first things first. Effective management is discipline, carrying it out."
—— Stephen R. Covey

Stephen R. Covey
Stephen Covey is an American educator, author, businessperson and keynote speaker. His most popular book is *"The 7 Habits of Highly Effective People"*.

SKINNY PRINCIPLE #1

IT DOES MATTER

Yes. It does Matter.

Too many good supervisors and managers fail to achieve their full potential and miss great job and career growth opportunities because of five fundamental shortcomings:

1. They fail to take the time and make the effort necessary to understand the essential differences in their roles of both *managing* and *leading* within an organizational structure;

2. They fail to appreciate and prepare themselves with the leadership development training and insights vital to be successful in new leadership roles accepted within their organizations---new roles may require new skills;

3. They fail to create a clear and concise mental picture of what is required of themselves and their team members to meet the organization's expectations and ensure a "win".

4. They fail to document and effectively communicate their vision and expectations to their work teams and to all stakeholders within the organization; and

5. They fail to build and maintain the relationships needed within their teams, and the organization as a whole, in order to establish the level of respect and trust the job demands.

However, overcoming these shortcomings is very much in the reach of most supervisors and managers. It only requires the commitment of the time, focus and energy necessary to take the *leadership strengthening* actions required to be in a position to always *lead* and *win*.

Here is the synopsis of "Skinny" Principle #1.

SKINNY PRINCIPLE #1
It Does Matter

This Principle draws attention to the fundamental truth that your roles as the "Leader" and the "Manager" are two of the most critical roles within any organization. You can either strengthen or weaken the organization's chances for success. This Principle underscores the reality that while both roles are important, your role as the organization's "Leader" differs in approach, tone and expectations from your role as the organization's "Manager". Your ability to maintain the proper mindset, preparation and focus in each role can be the difference between winning and failing. The simplest way to think of what to keep in mind here is **"I should <u>manage</u> tasks, assets and deadlines and I should <u>lead</u> people, expectations and outcomes."**

THE WHAT

The "What" here is the fact that good supervisors and managers can become more effective leaders by taking the actions necessary to eliminate leadership shortcomings.

To get started, we suggest that you take at least the following actions:

1. Do what is necessary to create a mindset that embraces the fundamental differences between *managing* and *leading* within an organizational structure;

2. Develop a realistic action plan — including a clear vision, targets and expectations. This will help you *stay on track* and to more effectively *manage* all of the operational tasks, assets and deadlines associated with meeting expectations;

3. Develop a second, executable action plan that outlines your leadership strategy. It should detail what you *must do* and *when you must do it* in order to effectively *lead* your work team and all of the stakeholders that are instrumental to your success; and

4. Recognize that your leadership focus and responsibility should include direct reports *as well as* all of the members of the organization who will benefit from your success or will be impacted by your failure.

THE WHY

"Why" take these actions and proactively focus on eliminating your fundamental leadership shortcomings? The two primary reasons are:

1. Every assignment and work team will be unique and present unique challenges requiring the appropriate level of leadership thought and strategy; and

2. Without the proper *leadership* mindset and a plan, you can expect to be mediocre at best and to fail most of the time.

As you may have detected while reading this chapter's narrative, Marilynn was educated and experienced as well as determined to succeed. She also recognized early on that she had to do something about the unravelling situation between herself and her work team. However, Marilynn was not prepared to *manage* the roll out of a new organization and a new function, nor was she equipped to *lead* the new, youthful work team.

Shutting down her team members' communication channels and driving them to seek the empathy of other managers within her Agency, only added to her challenge. Marilynn didn't develop and share with her team, co-workers and Agency executives her vision, approach and plan for achieving her new organization's mission. Also, since she didn't get their "buy in" — she had no way of winning the confidence and trust she needed to succeed.

By not recognizing, what her friend recognized and shared with her at the end of the story, *"It sounds like to me that your actions and thinking are those of a manager and not a leader"*, she was faced with the near impossible task of turning the situation around and succeeding.

THE HOW

Unlike the manager in this chapter's narrative, you don't have to accidentally run into an old friend to figure out what's going wrong. However, not having a plan to succeed − *now that you are aware of what's required* − is a plan to fail.

We suggest the following as a good start to "How" to eliminate leadership shortcomings.

1. First, outline both your management and your leadership action plan. Then, fill in the details as your management and leadership strategies evolve. Remember, the plans should address two similar yet diverse sets of job responsibilities − one for *managing* and one for *leading*;

2. Take the time to size-up the entire organization that hired or selected you as their leader. Your assessment should include all levels of the organization, including the corporate level. This exercise does not have to be done in secret. Let people know that you would like to become as familiar as possible with the organization's mission, history, culture, current operational strategy and future plans. The insights you gain here can be invaluable in your preparation to *lead* and *win*;

3. Learn as much as possible about the team you will lead. The organization's Human Resources Department may be able to share with you some important insights regarding your new team's make-up, experience levels and past performance records. If you are replacing the most recent

manager, find out why he or she left the organization and his or her performance challenges; and

4. Don't hesitate to update or change your plans. Remember, the only constant in life is change.

Your preparation and capacity to *lead* and *win* in your current or your next leadership role may require you to obtain or strengthen some specific management and/or leadership skills. Don't be fearful of getting better. You may have the opportunity to include some additional training, professional coaching or mentorship into your Position Acceptance Letter or Employment Contract.

THE WHEN

As in any major endeavor in life, success becomes more likely when "good preparation" meets a "great opportunity". As this chapter's narrative highlights, not being prepared to take on an immediate leadership challenge can leave you feeling defeated and like a loser. In terms of the "When" here, we suggest that you:

1. Immediately do what it takes to create a mindset that embraces the difference between *managing* and *leading*; and

2. Practice your ability to manage and to lead *today* as you perform the responsibilities of your current job or at home or within volunteer organizations.

As you develop and execute your management and leadership strengthening plans, you should use your intuition to guide the proper timing and pace associated in the execution of each action.

The key is to be constantly aware of every "on the job" situation that requires your personal involvement and − before you act or respond − first, decide if your *management acumen* or your *leadership prowess* would generate the best outcome.

IMPORTANT THINGS TO KEEP IN MIND

✓ Management uses structure, rules and processes in order to control and predict results in a stable environment.

✓ Leadership is about making a difference for all the people following you. When you fail as a leader, your people also fail. Leadership matters because people matter.

✓ *"If you are leading others and you're lonely, then you're not doing it right. Think about it. If you're all alone, that means nobody is following you. And if nobody is following you, then you're not really leading."* --John Maxwell

MANAGER VERSUS LEADER

Leadership and Management are two distinct however paired disciplines. Both are necessary to *lead* and *win*. You should keep the following Manager versus Leader *Action Comparisons* top of mind.

A MANAGER	A LEADER
Tells	**Sells**
This is what I want you to do, and here is how I want you to do it.	I have this great idea and I know it will work if I can get you to be a part of it.
Minimizes Risk	**Takes Risks**
Time is money. The sooner I get this done, the better.	This might stretch us, but the payoff will make it worthwhile.
Instructs	**Encourages**
If you're not sure of what your job entails, you can check the flowchart on my door.	If you think you have a better way, my door is always open.
Approves	**Motivates**
You did your job well and on time.	You know, I have never had to worry about you doing your job and doing it well.
Establishes Rules	**Breaks Rules**
Stick to the script. We can't have everyone just running around doing their own thing.	What are we doing that holds our team members back?
Relies on Control	**Inspires Trust**
My team members know the consequences if they get out of line.	My team members know I trust them to be the best they can be.
Does Things Right	**Does the Right Things**
Rules are rules. As much as I would like to, I can't make an exception.	I know what the rules say. But sometimes you just need to break them.

WHAT OTHERS ARE THINKING

"Do you want to know who you are? Don't ask. Act! Action will delineate and define you."
— Thomas Jefferson

Thomas Jefferson

Thomas Jefferson was an American Founding Father who was the principal author of the Declaration of Independence and later served as the third President of the United States from 1801 to 1809. Previously, he had been elected the second Vice President of the United States, serving under John Adams from 1797 to 1801.

CHAPTER TWO

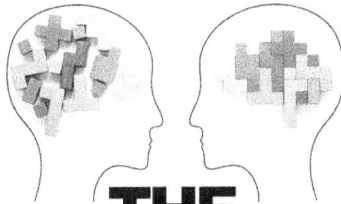

THE
SMART
LEADER
AND THE "SKINNY" PRINCIPLES

WHAT YOU DO BECOMES WHO YOU ARE

WHAT OTHERS ARE THINKING

"Authenticity and knowing who you are is fundamental to being an effective and long-standing leader."
— Ann Fudge

Ann Marie Fudge
Ann Fudge has served on a number of corporate boards, including those of General Electric, Novartis, Unilever and Infosys, as well as on several non-profit boards. She is former chairman and CEO of Young & Rubicam Brands, a global network of marketing communications companies.

A Situational Narrative

I THOUGHT THEY REALLY KNEW ME

It was around 12:45 PM on Wednesday afternoon and Mark Ashford has just returned from lunch. He intentionally returned a little early so that he could find a seat at the table near the rear of the large conference room.

Today is the big day. This afternoon he will finally receive the anxiously anticipated *"letters from home"*. This confidential feedback will give Mark a deeper appreciation of how his managers, a few co-workers and some subordinates perceive his leadership skills and behaviors. It should confirm his perception of how his organization views his leadership ability and set the stage for his elevation to vice president.

Mark was one of forty-five managers from companies located throughout the United States and Canada attending the five-day, internationally admired Senior Leadership Development Program (SLDP) offered by the Creative Leadership Academy.

Mark was not surprised his manager, Jack Kerry, selected him to attend this type of prestigious development program. He joined Medco Technologies ten years ago as a Senior Project Manager.

He had just added a PMP certification to his academic credentials, which include an engineering degree and an MBA. Mark was promoted a year ago to the role of the company's Corporate Manager of Project Management. Historically, the position has been a stepping-stone for being elevated to vice president. The recent promotion gave Mark the opportunity, for the first time, to lead a functional organization within Medco and to spend time with other department managers.

Due to the total cost of this pristine leadership development program, including the travel from Chicago to San Diego, it required the approval of the company's President, Durrell Billis.

Both Jack and Mr. Billis had attended the SLDP earlier in their careers and thought that it was one of the best programs of its type in North America. They valued the SLDP's intensity and the assessment tools used to help participants individually grasp important insights regarding their current leadership skills, behaviors and shortcomings based on anonymous feedback from key members within their organizations.

One unique aspect of the SLDP is the team of carefully chosen career psychologist brought in to spend four full hours with each participant on the fourth day of the Program.

The timing was important because on the third day of the Program, the training facilitator would provide each participant the results and feedback from a 360-degree Leadership Assessment. Each Program participant is required to complete and return the fully completed assessment package at least 30 days prior to the start of the Program.

Shortly after 1:15 PM, the big conference room was now full of participants and the Program facilitator entered the room with a stack of thick envelopes. The third day of the Program was always on a Wednesday and had become known as *"reality check Wednesday"*. The feedback from the 360-degree Leadership Assessment was jokingly referred to as the *"letters from home"*.

There were stories of how some past SLDP participants were so surprised by the feedback from their organization that they left the Program before the Friday close. Some even suffered nervous breakdowns and others later unexpectedly left their companies and management careers prematurely.

However, Mark was confident that he would get good results and positive feedback. He felt he was a natural leader. The reason he wanted a seat near the rear of the room this afternoon was to watch the reactions on the faces of other participants as they opened their *"letters from home"*.

As the SLDP facilitator approached his seat, Mark noticed that the expression on her face was one of concern. As he opened his envelope, he went straight to the anonymous feedback sections at the end of the purposefully arranged package.

The feedback was separated into three categories labeled: *"From Your Management"*, *"From Your Co-workers"* and *"From Your Subordinates"*. On the cover page of each category was a scoring bar, which ranged from 10% to 100%, representing the percentile of positive responses based on the Program's 23-year history of ranking Program participant feedback. Participants whose ranking were less than 50% were considered at risk and in need of significant improvement in their leadership skills and behaviors.

To Mark's bewilderment, he noticed that his ranking for each feedback category was less than 50%. As he slowly sank down into his chair, he said to himself, *"I thought they really knew me".*

Tonight, he would be required to agonizingly read the complete assessment and disappointing feedback from his organization. He left the conference room that afternoon wondering what had gone wrong. He wondered what he would say to the career psychologist that he was scheduled to spend time with on Thursday afternoon.

After a long and sleepless night of tossing and turning, Mark walked into a small meeting room Thursday afternoon where he found a middle-aged man named Joel Collins waiting. Joel was the career psychologist that had been assigned to work with Mark. Joel introduced himself and indicated that he had thoroughly reviewed Mark's assessment results and feedback. Joel suggested that they start their time together by having Mark respond to a few leadership patterns and behaviors that he had identified while analyzing the feedback from Mark's managers, co-workers and subordinates. Mark agreed and said in a dejected voice, *"Joel, I must admit that I am extremely disappointed. I thought they really knew me".*

Joel gently responded with, *"I know you are disappointed Mark. But, based on my professional analysis of all your assessment results as well as the level of detail in your feedback, I believe that, as a leader, they may know you better than you know yourself."*

Then, Joel initiated their counseling and coaching session with the following set of questions. Understandably, Mark's responses were somewhat emotional. Nevertheless, he was determined to respond to each question as honest and truthful as possible.

Joel: *Since you moved into your current "functional" management role from your "matrixed" project management role, have you felt a need to adjust your leadership approach?*

Mark: No. I was a successful Project Manager. All my current managers know my reputation and what I have done in the past. What I did to successfully lead my project teams as a Project Manager is what I plan to do in my new role — given enough time.

Joel: *Okay. It looks like you have been in your new position for about a year now. Have you been as successful in your new role as Corporate Manager of Project Management as you were in your prior position?*

Mark: Well, I must admit that the first six months or so were a little rocky and some things have gone wrong. However, I am sure that Jack and Mr. Billis understand that it will take a while for me to get up the learning curve. However, I do feel that I have done a decent job so far. They should have given me a break in their feedback.

Joel: *Okay. Have you met with all your current direct reports to learn what they think about you and the direction you are taking the* *organization? Have you taken the time to share with your entire team "who you are" and what they should expect from you as their new leader?*

Mark: No. Not yet. However, it's on my list. Nevertheless, my new team should realize that it will take time for them to get use to me and my leadership style. I have not had a chance to do any of those things. But I will get around to it.

Joel spent the remainder of their time together walking Mark through all the assessment results. He also took the time to give Mark his professional opinions on the numerous comments included in the Assessment feedback from his managers, co-workers, and subordinates.

After about three and a half hours, Mark began to realize that Joel was correct. Based on *what he had done* to date and the *actions* and *inaction* his organization had witnessed since he accepted the new leadership role, *"they did know him better than he knew himself."*

WHAT OTHERS ARE THINKING

"What you are will show in what you do.
— Thomas A. Edison

Thomas A. Edison

Thomas Alva Edison was an American inventor and businessperson, who has been described as America's greatest inventor. He is credited with developing many devices in fields such as electric power generation, mass communication, sound recording, and motion pictures.

SKINNY PRINCIPLE #2

WHAT YOU DO BECOMES
WHO YOU ARE

T he bottom line is that leadership is not about what you have done, what you plan to do or what you say. Leadership and being perceived by others in your organization as a leader will be centered on your actions. Who you are, as a leader, is about "what you do".

It is all about your actions, which includes —your deeds, how you treat others, how you make decisions, how you listen to others, how you accept responsibility for your actions and hold yourself accountable. As a new leader, w*hat you do will very quickly become who you are* in the eyes of others in your organization.

There are six fundamental shortcomings that many leaders fail to address in this area. We believe all leaders striving to become more effective and respected should avoid the following:

1. Misunderstanding their new role and responsibilities as the manager and *leader* when moving into a new position within their current or in a new organization.

2. Assuming that the team they are to lead and manage really know who they are — *You should tell your own story*.

3. Not taking the time and making the effort to get to know all of their team members as *individuals* and not just as subordinates.

4. Not effectively communicating with all of their team members and not passionately emphasizing their own role in and commitment to achieving the organization's mission, goals and objectives.

5. Making commitments and/or decisions they don't intend to keep — *Not walking your talk*; and

6. Assuming that they are the "smartest people in the room".

It is important to realize that all leaders — first time and experienced — at some point will make mistakes. It is also often true that making a mistake in a leadership role can be a learning opportunity and that "redemption" is possible. But then again, redemption must involve others who believe in second chances.

However, taking the time to learn how to recognize and avoid these six major shortcomings is best. By doing so, "you" will always be in the driver's seat while leading your organization and achieving its mission, goals and objectives.

Here is the synopsis of "Skinny" Principle #2.

SKINNY PRINCIPLE #2
What You Do Becomes Who You Are

This Principle draws attention to the fundamental truth that as the leader of your organization, "what you do", "when you do it" and the "results you achieve" are the major factors that determine "who you are" in the eyes, judgment and perception of your team and all others who matter. Also, "doing nothing" when action is required focuses an even brighter spotlight on a leader's lack of competency. The simplest way to think of what to keep in mind here is **"If I am asked to lead, I should always be authentic and do absolutely everything within my power to win. If I win, I am a winner with nothing to prove. If I fail, I am a failure with everything to prove."**

THE WHAT

The "What" in this case is the fact that, as your organization's leader, you have the responsibility and obligation to take the timely actions required to deliver the level of leadership your organization needs and deserves. It is your *actions* or *inaction* that will determine "who you are" in the eyes, judgement and perception of your team and all others who matter within your organization.

THE WHY

"Why" take such actions and focus on eliminating these fundamental leadership shortcomings? It's about the need to be "studious" and "proactive" in order to be an effective leader in today's complex, uncertain and dynamic environments. You should always keep in mind these four fundamental truths.

1. Being studious as a leader allows you to see more than others see, see farther than the others see, and see things before the others see them. This is a necessity. This type of vision is what all leaders need to always be in the position to be *proactive*.

2. Both for-profit and non-profit organizations today face environments, which are similar in complexity, uncertainty and dynamics. Having a studious and effective leader becomes essential in such scenarios in order to provide the organization with the vision, direction and momentum needed.

3. Effective leaders use *being proactive* as a way to create the "cushion" needed to have the time required to evaluate options and gather the accurate information needed to make good decisions and take the appropriate actions; and

4. Effective leaders also know that they must quickly assess the organization's performance and wisely navigate both

the operational and political environments to be in the position to take the actions required to *lead* and *win.*

In this chapter's narrative, Mark concluded, only after spending hours with the career psychologist, that his organization *"knew him better than he knew himself."* Unfortunately, for many new and some experienced leaders, this type of *delayed performance recognition* is more often the *reality* versus the *exception.* Too many good supervisors and managers fail to take the time to assess a new organization's environment and take the actions required to be perceived as and to get the results of an effective leader.

Mark's somewhat naive assumptions were certainly not based upon the recognition of the significant differences between managing and leading in any "matrix" versus a "functional" organizational environment."

"What I did to successfully lead my program teams as a Project Manager is what I plan to do in my new role" and *"my new team should realize that it will take time for them to get use to me and my leadership style"*

Mark's flawed and misguided expectations indicated that he lacked the leadership thought, skills and competency needed to be an effective leader in his new position.

"All of my current managers know my reputation and what I have done in the past. I am sure that Jack and Mr. Billis understand that it will take a while for me to get up the learning curve and they should have given me a break in their feedback."

If Mark had been more "studious" and "proactive", he would have recognized that moving into a new leadership role must be accompanied with the proper level of organizational knowledge and the leadership ability required to take appropriate and timely actions.

THE HOW

We suggest the following as a good start to "How" to eliminate these six fundamental leadership shortcomings.

1. Complete a matrix of the leadership roles, responsibilities and expectations of your current job. Then, list the knowledge, skills and temperament required for you to be effective in this leadership position. If you are not sure you have all the correct answers here, you should seek the help of a trusted mentor and/or leadership coach. We have included a *Leadership Role Evaluation Matrix Template* at the end of this chapter that can be helpful with this exercise.

2. Determine the most critical "deficits" and develop a realistic plan that you can execute to acquire the additional knowledge and skills. If there are serious temperament challenges, we suggest you consider finding a new position soon. Unfortunately, at most senior levels, conflicts associated with personality and leadership styles are normally insurmountable encounters.

3. If you haven't done so, get to know *as individuals* all of your team members who are within a couple of levels below you. Let your direct reports know that you would like to have what are called "two down" meetings with their direct reports, at least quarterly. Pick an interesting and current topic for each meeting. Remember, you should do most of the listening during these meetings. However, when the moment is right, you should take the opportunity to personally *"tell them your story"*.

4. Consider an "all hands" meeting with all the members of your organization, at least quarterly. Properly scheduled "virtual" meetings can conveniently serve this purpose. In each meeting, you should personally share and/or update your organization's mission, goals and objectives. Where

appropriate, you should discuss the specific roles that team members are expected to play in achieving them;

5. Develop a technique that will "trigger" a need for *caution* and prevent you from making a commitment until you are sure it is something that you can unconditionally deliver. Then, use the technique; and

6. As a leader of your organization, you should always keep this Confucius quote top of mind, *"If you are the smartest person in the room, then you are in the wrong room."*

THE WHEN

What you should do and "When" you should do it is best determined by a good ninety-day leadership plan.

New and expanding leadership roles can be exhilarating as well as overpowering. Regardless of the organizational structure, within the first ninety days, you must prove yourself as an asset to your organization.

The first ninety days is the period that you will be analyzed by the senior management team, your co-workers and your team members. Not only will the actions you take or fail to take determine "who you are" as a leader, but they will influence how others perceive your ability to be successful in your new role.

We suggest you create a ninety-day plan prior to moving into the new job or as soon after as possible after you are in the new position. This period is a vital time for you to gain traction and score some early wins. Here are some points to help guide you.

1. Be as visible as possible throughout the organization and when the opportunity reveals itself, *tell your story*.

2. Spend the appropriate amount of time with superiors, co-workers and team members and get to know them as *individuals*.

3. Determine where there are organizational weaknesses and where your new organization's performance may have been lacking in the past.

4. Empower others to open-up to you by gaining their trust through your authenticity — *be who you are.*

5. Welcome and accept all feedback. Listen. Learn. Act.

Leadership Role Evaluation Matrix Template

The knowledge, skills and temperament required to be successful.

	Knowledge	Skills	Temperament
My Leadership Role In general, my leadership role is....			
My Responsibilities In general, my responsibilities are...			
My Team Member Expectations In general, my Team expects me to...			
My Management Expectations In general, my Management expect me to...			

What are my critical deficits in knowledge, skills and temperament?
Deficit = *What I need* versus *What I currently have*

How will I address the critical deficits? (What, Why, How and When)

CHAPTER THREE

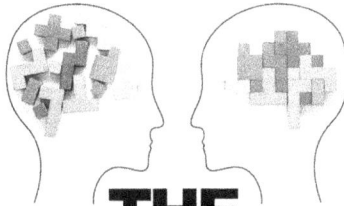

THE SMART LEADER

AND THE "SKINNY" PRINCIPLES

WHERE YOU SPEND YOUR TIME IS NOT YOUR CHOICE

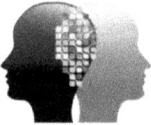

WHAT OTHERS ARE THINKING

"It's not enough to be busy, so are the ants. The question is, what are we busy about?" — Henry David Thoreau

Henry David Thoreau

Henry David Thoreau was an American essayist, poet, philosopher, abolitionist, naturalist, tax resister, development critic, surveyor, yogi, and historian.

A Situational Narrative

I WAS BORN TO DO THIS

My Dad loved reproducing antique furniture and he started our family business in his woodworking shop. When the "naked oak" craze was all the rage in the 1970's, Dad took the family savings and invested in unfinished "naked oak" furniture.

It didn't take long for my Dad, Julius Lane, to realize that people loved the idea of doing it themselves. Therefore, once they saw Dad's pieces, they were happy to purchase the furniture kits and thrilled about the idea of DIY.

As the retail part of the business expanded, Dad cut back on his own woodworking and hired four full time furniture makers and two apprentices for the shop. Soon, over fifty percent of Lane's Fine Custom Furnishings retail sales were custom antique reproduction kits. The remaining sales were from our custom, "unfinished" line. The "naked oak" phase eventually died off, but customers kept returning to say hello, browse and purchase our customized furniture and furniture kits.

A few years later, Dad invested in a large warehouse and storefront. It was on a corner lot located on North Hayden Road and Thomas in Old Town Scottsdale, Arizona — where it stands today.

Dad started scanning the country, contracting with other artisans to add uniquely designed furniture and accessories to the store's growing inventory.

I'm CeCe Lane and from the time I saw my first antique reproduction, I knew my life would always involve art and furniture.

At the age of twelve, I was sketching furniture designs and sourcing pieces for the store. When I entered my teens, Dad let me pick several new pieces of furniture. Most never sold, like the turtle coffee table and pelican lamp. After two years on the floor, Dad just removed the price tags from those two pieces and made them our store "mascots."

They later became a running joke between the staff and me.

Art and history are in my blood, so naturally I majored in art history in college. While in college, I thoroughly enjoyed the campus life. However, I missed my daily visits to the store and being in the comfort of the retail environment. I would go into the store while on college breaks and the salesclerks would always rib me with a greeting, "CeCe, I almost sold the turtle coffee table today!"

I have always considered myself a part of the Lane's Fine Custom Furnishings family. However, it was a big surprise when Dad offered me a job. Initially, I thought he was just being generous.

He certainly didn't have to put me on the payroll. After all, I started contributing my designs when I was twelve and I was continuing to be an active part of the design team.

Then, Dad added, *"I think it's time for me to start grooming you to one-day take a leadership role in the business."* This was even a bigger surprise. I did believe that I was becoming an incredibly good designer, but I never felt that I would be particularly good at running the business.

By 2000, seventy percent of Lane's Fine Custom Furnishings sales revenue came from our own customized design and antique reproduction furniture lines. A larger percentage of the orders were now requiring shipping across the country. Fortunately, Dad was exceptionally good at managing production and packaging costs. Therefore, even when sales required shipping, Lane's retail prices, including shipping cost, were always competitive.

In 2001, Lane's Fine Custom Furnishings published its first product and sales catalog. The catalog was easily adapted to what is now Lane's online presence. Like almost everything related to the real estate and housing market between 2006 and 2009, Lane's business was critically impacted by the Great Recession. Lane's survived the crash and stayed afloat. It was all due to my Dad's ability to minimize inventory levels, control raw materials cost and obtain short-term financing to support cash flow.

Our core staff stayed with us through the "crash" and by 2014, Lane's sales revenue was on an upswing. Dad was able to add a full-time designer, a sales manager and two part-time retail salesclerks. He also developed a contract relationship with a retail marketing firm to update the store sales and marketing strategy.

Just after Dad watched me graduate with my PhD in Art History from the University of Arizona, he told me he was thinking about selling the business. I almost fell off my Wegner reproduction.
I hated the thought of selling our family business. I guess I thought Lane's would go on forever. Dad shared that the only option to not selling would be for me to take over the business. I said, *"Dad, I love Lane's. But surely you know my designer's eye would not be enough to run our family business."*

Dad just smiled and said, *"CeCe, you were born to do this."*

It did seem to be the perfect time for me to take over Lane's Fine Custom Furnishings. The new home and construction industry were growing again, and our customer base was expanding. However, in the past, while spending much of my life in the store, I just couldn't seem to figure out the business side of things.

After some serious consideration, I told Dad I would give it a try. Therefore, after all the years of working around the business, I started my first official apprenticeship — to learn how to be successful at running the business.

My Dad just hung back for the first few weeks, allowing me to "get the feel" for the job. I had no problem getting acquainted with the market strategy and big picture of the furniture business. I also quickly began to understand each of the many moving parts of the business operations. However, figuring out how to make them work together to become a successful enterprise became more and more challenging. As I began to get more involved in day-to-day activities, I was beginning to really lose confidence in what I was doing. I also began to seriously doubt if I could really do this.

From a distance, Dad made it all look easy. But, after only a few months, I was ready to quickly return to teaching and designing. However, the thought of a future without Lane's Fine Custom Furnishings was even more frightening.

Feeling a little frustrated and confused, I went to Dad with the "white towel" in hand.

Dad said, *"CeCe. It takes time to learn how to make it all work. I'm glad it looked like it was easy, but it was just experience and some key time management skills. Let's try something different."*

For the next six months, I worked closely with Dad. I shadowed him as he went about managing and leading every aspect of the business. I watched him as he managed the retail operations, attracted new customers, gained repeat business, controlled inventory, managed cash flow and kept the entire staff motivated.

The most time-consuming efforts appeared to be associated with how Dad masterfully interfaced with the material wholesalers and how he was able to connect with the mostly remote team members handling online customer orders.

One night at dinner, I said to him, *"Dad, it's amazing to see how you seem to always be in the right place at just the right time."*

My Dad replied, *"Yes, my dear, that does appear to be one of my best acts."*

After about a year and a half, I was fully in charge of all business operations. Two years after that, my Dad officially retired and I finally became the new owner and leader of Lane's Fine Custom Furnishings. Over the next five years, there were some ups and downs, but the business grew at a manageable rate and was profitable.

While shadowing my Dad and learning the "skinny" of how to run a small business, I learned some key and incredibly important lessons from him — such as how to be a "good manager" and how to balance the "ebb and flow" of a retail sales organization.

My Dad's gift of providing sound advice also continued to be amazing. There is one special piece of advice that I received from him regarding my responsibility as both a business owner and a "good leader" that I will never forget.

The special piece of advice was for me to remember that, as a leader, *"where you spend your time is not your choice, it's your responsibility."*

Thanks to my amazing Dad and his trust in me, I now realize that *"I was born to do this".*

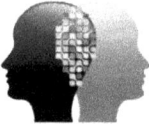

WHAT OTHERS ARE THINKING

"Time management is an oxymoron. Time is beyond our control, and the clock keeps ticking regardless of how we lead our lives. Priority management is the answer to maximizing the time we have." — John C. Maxwell

John C. Maxwell

John Calvin Maxwell is an American author, speaker, and pastor who has written many books, primarily focusing on leadership. Titles include *"The 21 Irrefutable Laws of Leadership"* and *"The 21 Indispensable Qualities of a Leader"*. His books have sold millions of copies, with some on the New York Times Best Seller List.

SKINNY PRINCIPLE #3

WHERE YOU SPEND YOUR TIME IS NOT YOUR CHOICE

Time is one of life's constants that we are all given. No one in your organization gets more or less of it than anyone else. However, as the leader of the organization, everyone wants and needs "your" time.

Most good managers and supervisors generally know how they should spend their time. They also know that what they choose to prioritize reveals what's important to them and ultimately will determine their organization's outcomes. It's a lesson that is taught and learned by managers and supervisors in basic management or supervisory training.

But, there is one lesson that seems to consistently be missed or forgotten. That is, as the organization's leader, where you spend your time is not your "choice". Having a method to sense where to best spend your time at any given moment and during any situation is one of your primary "responsibilities".

Here are five fundamental shortcomings that limit the ability of good managers and supervisors to sense where to best spend their time:

1. Not knowing how to gauge the "temperature" and feeling of what's happening within their organization.

2. Not knowing how to anticipate problems, troublesome situations and potential conflict in a timely fashion;

3. Not knowing how to interject their skills and experience into problem solving without being viewed as owning the issue.

4. Not knowing when their presence is required to ensure the desired outcome.

5. Not being comfortable with having "uncomfortable" interventions and conversations when the situation demands it.

Here is the synopsis of "Skinny" Principle #3.

SKINNY PRINCIPLE #3

Where You Spend Your Time Is Not Your Choice

This Principle draws attention to the fundamental truth that as the leader of the organization, everyone wants and needs your time. Where you spend it, is "not your choice but your responsibility". It is your responsibility to make sure that your time is allocated wisely. Most effective leaders spend the majority of their time in three key areas: 1) Where they can prevent a pending crisis 2) Where, without their presence, a crisis can't be resolved to the organization's best interest or 3) Where they sense a real need for encouragement, empathy or additional resources. The simplest way to think of what to keep in mind here is **"As a leader, I should spend the vast amount of my time where my presence can make an undeniable difference in achieving organizational goals. I should ask myself at the time, do I feel a little outside of my comfort zone here. If the answer is yes, then I know that — where I am — is where I should be."**

THE WHAT

The "What" here is the reality that the time you spend within your organization is the only constant. Thus, when a leader is not in the "right" place at the "right" time, the "opportunity lost" is irreversible.

If you don't currently have a proven method or technique to sense where to best spend your time at any given moment and during any situation, you are not fulfilling a critical role that your organization requires of you.

THE WHY

The "Why" here is based on the reality that, as your organization's leader, when you spend the vast amount of your time where your presence can make an undeniable difference, it will:

1. Improve your leadership effectiveness and efficiency.

2. Ensure that your time is being spent on activities that are important and critical to your organization's success; and

3. Minimize the number of urgent activities — by doing so, you will minimize the stress throughout the organization associated with "fighting fires" and chasing last minute deadlines.

THE HOW

Our experiences and the experiences of those we have researched have led us to believe that an organizational leader's time is not something that can be saved — it can only be spent more or less wisely.

"How" can you more wisely spend your time? Of course, specific steps will heavily depend upon you, your current situation, your organizational alignment and your organizational culture.

However, we suggest that the first step should be to train and empower your team members to utilize good business processes and make wiser decisions on a daily basis. When the decision-making and business execution process are improved throughout the organization, you will have more time to identify potential problem areas. You will also have more time to spend on activities where your presence can make an undeniable difference.

Here are some time management tools that many senior leaders use to help them know if they are spending their time on the right issues and to preserve their time for areas where their presence can make the most difference.

1. They spend more time with their team leads. This helps them gauge the "temperature" and gain more insight into what's really happening within their organization.

2. They use the art of focused and discipline agenda setting to help establish and communicate priorities. This helps to eliminate unnecessary meetings.

3. They measure the real value of every item on the agenda and allocate their time accordingly. They work toward getting issues off the agenda as quickly as possible.

4. They structure top management meetings to drive and produce real decisions and not just meet to schedule another meeting.

THE WHEN

"When" should you start to *always be in the right place at just the right time?* We suggest that you start as soon as you establish or refine your technique for sensing where to best spend your time within your organization.

Just as CeCe in this chapter's narrative shadowed her Dad in order to gain real insight and an appreciation of how *he made it all look easy*, you may need to find a mentor within your organization or discipline who has figured it all out and learn from him or her.

But, by all means, do it now. You and your organization will reap the rewards of you fulfilling your responsibility in this area.

CHAPTER FOUR

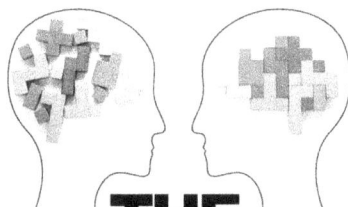

THE
SMART
LEADER
AND THE "SKINNY" PRINCIPLES

THE CARDS YOU PLAY WILL
DETERMINE WHO WINS

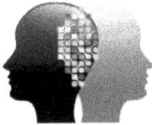

WHAT OTHERS ARE THINKING

"A leader's job is not to do the work for others, it's to help others figure out how to do it themselves, to get things done, and to succeed beyond what they thought possible.
—Simon Sinek

Simon Sinek

Simon Sinek is a leadership guru, professor at Columbia University, founder of SinekPartners (Corporate Refocusing) and author. He is best known for popularizing the concept of *"the golden circle"* and to *"Start With Why"*. Simon Sinek is also an adjunct staff member of the RAND Corporation.

A Situational Narrative

I SIMPLY PLAYED THE CARDS I WAS DEALT

My name is Sara Hornbill, and I am the CEO of a multi-national specialty products company. With over 1,500 retail sales locations throughout the Americas, Canada and most of the European Union, Walbash International, operates on narrow profit margins. We have hundreds of direct competitors who are constantly seeking to take market share.

For us, the key to staying financially afloat in any region is the ability of each location's General Manager to negotiate a reduced wholesale purchase cost for our products and to win competitive bids on mega-quantities of bestselling products and top brands.

I consider myself an empathetic leader, but rarely do I ask any of my General Managers to visit me in our corporate office in New York City and take the time out of their busy schedules to share with me how they orchestrated a big win or a suffered a big lost.

However, I considered this unique situation worthy of such an unusual request. I invited Alex Vanberry to join me in my office a few weeks ago for a postmortem review on how he and his Portugal-based team were able to successfully negotiate one of the largest mega-quantity wins and business turnarounds in our company's fifteen-year history.

Alex joined Walbash International four years ago with proven management skills but with only a few years of global retail sales experience.

When he accepted the General Manager's role in Lisbon last year, the location was operating at a financial lost and needed to quickly revamp its product line and win new market share to survive.

This could only be achieved by winning competitive bids for new name brand products that were available and selling like hotcakes throughout the EU.

Due to budget constraints, Alex was only allowed to take with him to Lisbon a couple of senior retail professionals he had known in his previous assignments. Thus, with this limitation, he would have to utilize the existing staff to achieve some challenging goals and to prevent Walbash International from shutting down the location.

When Alex walked into my New York office for our meeting, I had four questions prepared to ask and to probe into his recent accomplishments.

My questions were based on my keen knowledge of the situation and work environment he walked into when he accepted the Lisbon job. I thought that by asking him this set of specific questions, we could cut to the chase. My goal was to quickly gain an understanding of whether this *amazing feat* could be replicated in other Walbash International locations.

The first question I asked Alex was:

What did you perceive as your top challenge in your new role doing the first few weeks on the job?

Alex's reply was:

> *"Well, since I was going into a situation with only two team members that I was familiar with, I quickly realized that I was technically the new guy on the block.*
>
> *Therefore, I perceived my top challenge as the need to become familiar with the team members I inherited and who had to do the work required*

for us to achieve the company goals. I spent most of my time the first few weeks getting to know each of my team members. I wanted to know their strengths, their weaknesses, their fears and what they needed from me to be successful.

I felt that if I could put myself in their shoes, I would be able to understand the <u>cards</u> <u>I</u> <u>had</u> <u>to</u> <u>play</u>, if you will, to have a chance to turn things around and get some much-needed wins."

The second question I asked was:

How did you determine what your primary role should be as the leader of an organization burdened with such financial and organizational challenges?

Alex's reply was:

"That was easy. Once I determined that the staff I had inherited was an experienced team, I spent the time to listen to them. Their assessment of our current business challenges was quite insightful. Then, when I learned that they were well schooled in negotiating with the local product wholesaler community and familiar the new products we needed to revamp the product line, I just had to make sure of two things. First, I had to ensure the entire team understood my turn-around strategy. Secondly, I had to clearly share with them what I expected from each of them and what I was willing to do to help them be successful."

The third question I asked was:

In your opinion, what was missing in the organization when you arrived and how may it have contributed to the organization's poor performance?

Alex's reply was:

In my opinion, what was sorely missing was an adequate level of senior leadership presence. By this I mean, someone who understood and accepted the fact that his or her job was <u>not</u> to <u>do</u> <u>the</u> <u>work</u>, but to understand the capabilities of each team member and to make sure that they "all" were in the best position to win and deliver the results needed.

The final question I asked Alex was:

In a few words, how would you summarize the approach you used to lead your team to such a high level of success?

Alex's reply was:

> *"Well, with limited staffing options and mounting challenges, I was forced to be a leader and not just a manager. I quickly recognized that winning within an organizational structure is indeed a team sport.*
>
> *Organizationally, I needed them, and they needed me.*
>
> *Therefore, I committed the time to get to know each team member's capabilities, strengths, and weaknesses as well as the role I needed to play to get the most out of each member's contribution to achieving our goals.*
>
> *From there, as the game of winning bids for key products and successfully increasing product sales unfolded, I simply played the cards I was dealt."*

In hindsight, what I gained from my postmortem review with Alex Vanberry was a decisive affirmation of the fact that the fundamentals of what it takes to be an effective leader and to get consistently outstanding organizational results are rather basic.

However, a manager's ability to recognize the significant value of these leadership fundamentals and to effectively apply and benefit from them is the true leadership challenge.

I was also reminded of how difficult a task it would be for me to replicate Alex's *amazing feat* without having more leaders like Alex in the organization.

SKINNY PRINCIPLE #4

THE CARDS YOU PLAY WILL
DETERMINE WHO WINS

Recognizing and effectively fulfilling your leadership role and responsibilities in the context of the organizational structure can make the difference between winning and losing.

However, as what Sara Hornbill learned in this chapter's narrative, *"the fundamentals of what it takes to be an effective leader and to get consistently outstanding organizational results are rather basic"*. The true leadership challenge is a manager or supervisor's ability to recognize the value of these leadership fundamentals and to effectively apply them.

When you are facing unique business and organizational challenges, it is imperative that you remember that your job, as the organization's leader, is not to "do the work". Your team members have that job and responsibility.

As the organization's leader, it is your job and primary responsibility to understand the capabilities, strengths, and weaknesses of each of your team members. Then, you must leverage these valuable insights to get the most out of each member's contribution to winning and achieving organizational goals.

Very seldom will you be in a position to cherry-pick all of the members of your staff and your work team. Your leadership role requires that you do everything that is necessary to understand the *"hand that you have been dealt"* and make sure that all of your *"cards"* —aka team members— are in the best position to contribute to getting a win.

The raw reality is that regardless of the organizational or business challenge, in the end, the cards you play will determine who wins.

Here are seven fundamental shortcomings that we have found that many good managers and supervisors have when it comes to making sure that all of their team members are in the best position to contribute to the organization's success.

1. They fail to connect each team member's goals to larger organizational goals. For individual goals to be meaningful and effective, they must be tied to larger organizational goals.

2. They fail to make sure that each team member's goals are attainable but challenging based on individual capabilities and strengths.

3. They fail to create a personalized plan for each team member's success. You should ask each team member to explain how he or she will accomplish the assigned tasks.

4. They fail to build working relationships with each team member so that the team member feels comfortable asking for help when problems arise.

5. They fail to take the time required to understand and integrate a team member's personal interests into their professional goals.

6. They fail to encourage team members to act as "strength advocates" to help others use their talents and gifts more fully.

7. They fail to consider cross training among team members who have specific strengths.

Here is the synopsis of "Skinny" Principle #4.

SKINNY PRINCIPLE #4

The Cards You Play Will Determine Who Wins

This Principle draws attention to the fundamental truth that, as the leader, your job is not to "do the work". Your job is to get the expected organizational results. As the organization's leader, it's your job and responsibility to understand the capabilities of each of the *"cards"* — aka team members — you are dealt [provided or selected] and to make sure that they are "all" in the best position to win and deliver the expected results. This job is somewhat like playing a game of Solitaire. In the real world, just as in Solitaire, you don't get to handpick all of your "playing cards". However, you must "read the hand you are dealt" and determine what it takes to win by placing each team member in the best position within the organization to contribute to the organization's goals. The simplest way to think of what to keep in mind here is **"As my organization's leader, my responsibility is to get the expected organizational results and not to do the work of others. My job is to ensure that each team member is in the best position to deliver what is needed and has the resources required to ensure an organizational victory."**

THE WHAT

The "What" here is the need for managers and supervisors to understand, accept and successfully act upon the fact that, as the organization's leader, your job is not to *do the work*. Your job is to *get the expected organizational results*.

Your primary leadership responsibility is to spend the time required to understand and appreciate the capabilities of each team member and to make sure that they "all" are in the best position to win and deliver the desired results.

The typical shortcomings in this area can be more that adequately addressed by taking the following two important actions:

1. Consciously committing to work more closely with each member of your team to understand their weaknesses and appreciate their strengths.; and

2. Developing productive one-on-one working relationships with each team member.

THE WHY

The "Why" here is best summed up in the following Ken Blanchard quote:

> "Connect the dots between individual roles and the goals of the organization. When people see that connection, they get a lot of energy out of work. They feel the importance, dignity, and meaning in their job."— Ken Blanchard

The reality that you should remember is that if just one team member does not know you, respect you or trust your motives, your organization's overall performance suffers.

Of course, knowing all your team member's names and occasionally being in their presence at work can build some level of rapport. However, many surveys suggest that with just minimum contact, the average team member will still only perform at a level required to keep his or her job.

SMART leaders know that developing a positive and productive working relationship with each team member can help to bring their unique creativity and passion to the workplace. Acting upon this single and fundamental will release more minds seeking more solutions to problems or streamlining more processes within your organization.

THE HOW

We suggest you get started with the "How" here by spending more time to understand and embrace the leadership approach detailed by Alex Vanberry in this chapter's narrative. Here are some ideas to remember.

1. **Make it a priority to consciously get to know each of your team members as individuals.**

   Just the action of spending one-on-one time with a team member and demonstrating a sincere sense of professional empathy builds trust.

   You can use the *"Getting to Know You" Discussion and Discovery* exercise at the end of this chapter as a guide.

2. **Actively listen to each team member's assessment of his or her organizational role and current business challenges**.

   Remember, being an active listener not only means focusing on what your team member is saying but also actively showing verbal and non-verbal signs of listening.

   As you are aware, in both personal and professional life, listening is one of the most important skills that a leader must have. Being an active listener has a positive impact on your job effectiveness and the quality of your relationships with others.

3. **Be the leader of the communication between you and all members of your team. You should set the tone and do it often.**

   Effective and frequent communications by you, the organization's leader, develops trust, builds confidence, establishes an example and guards against unnecessary gossip and the consequential fear of not knowing.

THE WHEN

As we mentioned earlier, if even just one team member does not know you, respect you or trust your motives, your organization's overall performance suffers.

Therefore, "When" should you start to understand the capabilities, strengths, and weaknesses of each of your team members? Of course, the answer is the first day you are asked to become their leader.

Getting to Know You
A Team Member Discussion and Discovery Exercise

Objective: Get to know your team member.

Materials: Create a set of cards with each containing a single question.

Directions: You and your team member take turn pulling cards from a single deck and answering a question that corresponds with the card's face (see below). You should always follow their response with the comment and question — *Very interesting* and *Why?*

1- What is one of your hobbies?
2- What is one of your favorite colors?
3- What is one of your favorite foods?
4- What is one of your favorite music groups?
5- What is one of your dream jobs?
6- What is one of your favorite school subjects?
7- What is one of your favorite memories with your family?
8- What is one of your favorite animals?
9- What is one place you would love to travel someday?
10- What is one of your favorite books?
Jack- What is one thing you would like to improve about you?
Queen- What is one of your favorite TV shows?
King- What is one of your favorite movies?
Ace- What is one subject that you struggle with the most?
Joker- What is one interesting fact about you?

Remember: The idea is to get to know the team member and NOT to talk about work.

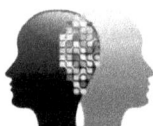

WHAT OTHERS ARE THINKING

"Leadership presence is the reflection of the leader's inner self. It should be the real deal. Presence, however, is not simply a sense of being; it is a determination of action."
- John Baldoni

John Baldoni
John Baldoni is the author of *"The Leader's Guide to Speaking with Presence: How to Project Confidence, Conviction, and Authority?"*

CHAPTER FIVE

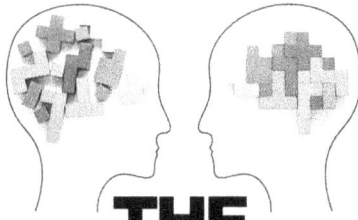

THE
SMART
LEADER
AND THE "SKINNY" PRINCIPLES

BEING PRESENT WITH YOUR PRESENCE

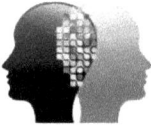

WHAT OTHERS ARE THINKING

"Enlightened leadership is spiritual if we understand spirituality not as some kind of religious dogma or ideology but as the domain of awareness where we experience values like truth, goodness, beauty, love and compassion, and also intuition, creativity, insight and focused attention."
—Deepak Chopra

Deepak Chopra
Deepak Chopra is an Indian-born American author, public speaker, alternative medicine advocate, and a prominent figure in the New Age movement. Through his books and videos, he has become one of the best-known and wealthiest figures in alternative medicine.

A Situational Narrative

AN ASTONISHING LACK OF LEADERSHIP PRESENCE

My long flight arrived in Charlotte, North Carolina at approximately eleven o'clock Thursday night. The flight from Phoenix was over four hours and fortunately, it was without any delays. It was after midnight by the time I collected my bag, caught a cab and checked into my downtown hotel room.

My wife and I lived in the Charlotte area for about seven years in the early 2000s. I was quite familiar with Charlotte's downtown development history and was eager to see what had changed over the past decade. However, there will not be any time this trip for a tour of the Queen City to satisfy my curiosity.

This is an unscheduled and unusual business trip and mission for me. This business trip only permits me to spend twenty-four hours here in Charlotte. My mission is to conduct a corporate investigation and to prepare a confidential report this weekend in support of a Monday morning deliverable commitment I made to a special client earlier this week.

My first meeting will start at seven in the morning and I will most likely not complete all my meetings and interviews until late in the evening. Why am I here, you ask? First, let me take the time to share with you a little background on myself and some basic, but important, insights into the disturbing, yet often repeated, organizational performance challenge I have been asked to investigate.

****

My name is Anthony Jerome McAdoo. Most people call me AJ.

I retired from my 30-year career in corporate America around ten years ago. My last corporate position was as a Senior Technology Manager and the Head of Data Center Management for the Capital Cargo Bank.

On Monday of this week, I attended an Executive Leadership Conference in San Francisco. While there, I met Ralph Dean, the new President and CEO of the Capital Cargo Bank. He moved into this role after I had left Capital Cargo in 2009. During a lunch conversation, I shared with Ralph a few highlights of my tenure with Capital Cargo. I also mentioned the fact that I was attending this special leadership conference because I am now an organizational leadership development consultant with a keen interest in helping leaders understand the true power of leadership.

I was somewhat surprised when Ralph asked if I could meet him for dinner that same evening. He wanted to discuss a somewhat mystifying organizational and business performance challenge he and the Capital Cargo executive team were currently facing. Not satisfied with the feedback he was receiving from a consultant he hired a few months ago, he indicated that he was interested in getting another perspective on the challenge. I said, *"Sure. It would be my pleasure."*

I met Ralph for dinner that evening around eight-thirty. I must admit that I was a little shocked with his degree of candor. I learned that he was genuinely concerned about a presentation he had to give to Capital Cargo Bank's Board of Directors in a meeting scheduled for next week. It turns out that Capital Cargo has experienced multiple outages of their online banking system over the past six months. All the outages were traced back to a critical Data Center located in Charlotte, North Carolina. The daylong outages were having a severely negative impact on

Capital Cargo's customer base and stock price. Any additional outages simply could not be tolerated.

Surprisingly, after several weeks of working with a consultant who was dispatched to Charlotte to determine the root cause of the problem, Ralph's executive team still could not provide him an explanation of the problem that he felt was adequate. In his words, *"The explanations I have been given to this point simply don't hold water; and can't be presented to my Board of Directors next Tuesday."*

After providing an hour-long breakdown of the situation and the most recent findings, Ralph asked if I could take a trip to the Charlotte Data Center and spend a day with the Data Center senior management team. He also asked if I would provide him a report detailing what I thought was the root cause of the problems and what might be a possible solution. He needed the report the following Monday.

Having a technical background, Ralph was less concerned with the feedback he had received regarding the technical issues and more concerned with what he perceived in his words, as *"a lack of senior leadership focus and organizational cohesiveness"*. Sensing that Ralph was sincerely interested in getting my perspective and that he would give my report a fair hearing, I agreed to modify my schedule to include a trip to Charlotte later in the week. The plan will be to learn about the root cause of Capital Cargo's situation and determine a possible solution.

****

Thus, here I am in Charlotte. As I mentioned earlier, tomorrow I will meet with the Charlotte Data Center management team. I also plan to meet with and interview as many of the members of the Charlotte work team as possible. My goal is to gain some operative insight into what is really happening at Capital Cargo's Charlotte Center, both operationally and organizationally. I intend to provide a report to Ralph Dean on Monday morning.

****

Well, it's early Saturday morning and I am back in my office in Phoenix working to complete the report I will deliver to Ralph Dean and Capital Cargo Monday morning. For about three hours now, I have been busy reviewing notes from my meetings and interviews. During my twenty-plus hours in Charlotte, I met with the entire Capital Cargo Data Center senior management team and interviewed all the key members of the technical and project staff. In summary, about half of what I discovered and observed was not surprising. However, the other half was quite disturbing.

First, here is the half that was not surprising.

The consolidation of four older regional data centers into the new Charlotte Data Center concluded about six months ago. Prior to this consolidation effort, Capital Cargo had not experienced a daylong outage of their online banking system in over 10 years.

When I arrived at the Charlotte Data Center Friday morning, the first thing I discovered was that, since the consolidation project's completion, most of the Charlotte team has been working through numerous problems with the installation of new server technology, the upgrade of old technology and a massive data migration effort. All of this was in addition to the normal activity associated with data center operations. Because of the magnitude of the consolidation effort and the new skill sets required to integrate the disparate systems, the project required a significant amount of leadership presence to sort through the available skills and competences of the Data Center's technical and project staff.

Based on my Data Center experience, I knew that the key to any successful consolidation effort of this type is to have a comprehensive integration strategy and work plans at all levels of the organization. Not surprising, throughout the data center facility, I found a dedicated and committed technical and project staff. They were working long hours and overtime was abundant. I have learned over the years that this situation frequently occurs at the end of most large system integration and data migration projects. Therefore, these initial findings were not a surprise.

However, it soon became apparent to me that the team's major challenges were three-fold: 1) the lack of a comprehensive problem resolution strategy; 2) the lack of an organizational-wide work plan; and 3) the lack of an adequate level of leadership presence. For me to discover major gaps in *strategic, tactical and operational leadership* — months after system "go live" — was quite unusual. The absence of attention and presence at all three of these levels of leadership in a corporation the size of Capital Cargo was unthinkable.

Now, here is the other half of what I discovered and observed at the Charlotte Data Center. This is the part that astonishingly, left me both surprised and quite disturbed.

Although the Capital Cargo Data Center senior management team included experienced technologist and managers, it was apparent during my visit that this particular team lacked the senior leadership skills required to lead such a complex and multi-facetted consolidation. The turnover rate of both the project management and technical staff had increased significantly over the last few months. After only a few hours at the Center, I could sense a general feeling of desperation at all levels of the organization. A couple of senior team leads shared with me during private interviews that, starting a few months ago, the sense of desperation seemed to have increased sharply. This was about the same time that most members of the middle management team began to feel that they *had to* and were *expected to* spend most of their time on the operations floor to help "do the work".

During my discussions with the team's project managers, I discovered that a few members of the senior management team did stay in the position to recognize global integration issues surrounding the consolidation project. They also had the authority to quickly shift or add the skills and resources required to resolve issues more proactively. However, after multiple requests by several project managers, they failed to do so.

In conclusion, it became clear to me that there was simply not a sufficient level of senior leadership presence throughout the Charlotte Data Center organization. Without such presence, it was nearly impossible to develop a winning level of cohesiveness, gain concurrence on an overall resolution strategy and create the organizational momentum required for the Charlotte Center to be successful — and outage free.

****

On Monday morning, I submitted what I believe was an honest and very comprehensive report to Ralph Dean and the Capital Cargo executive team, as promised.

The cover page of my report included:

Report on the Charlotte Data Center Performance Challenge

Root Cause: Senior Leadership Missing in Action

Solution: Leadership Training and/or New Leaders Needed

****

A few weeks later, while heading home from work, I received the following text message from Ralph Dean:

"Thanks, AJ. Good job. Just as I suspected. An astonishing lack of leadership presence. It was an extremely difficult Board meeting last month. New leadership team now in place at the Charlotte Data Center. Corporate-wide leadership training sessions will start soon."

SKINNY PRINCIPLE #5
BEING PRESENT WITH YOUR PRESENCE

Every team member impacts his or her organization's direction. However, your role as the organization's leader has by far the largest and most direct effect on organizational culture, cohesiveness and performance.

In contemporary leadership training, the expression *leadership presence* focuses on your ability to assume a leadership role throughout the organization, to share thinking and opinion with confidence and to strike a balance between talking and listening. All of which is to ensure that your communications are both persuasive and impactful.

In this chapter, our discussion of "being present" focuses on the simple fact that your organization needs you to be physically and mentally "present" and "involved" at all three levels of organizational leadership — *strategic, tactical and operational.*

As the leader, not being physically, mentally and emotionally "present" when it comes to the allocation of resources, the management of major risks and the validation of the corporate strategy is equivalent to you being seriously *missing in action.* Without exception, you must always be "present with your presence" in order to ensure that you — and your organization — are in the best position to always *lead* and *win.*

As concluded by AJ in this chapter's narrative, *"Without such presence, it is nearly impossible to develop a winning level of organizational cohesiveness, gain concurrence among your work teams on strategy and create the organizational momentum required to win."*

85

No. This does not mean that it is your job, as your organization's leader, to "do all the work". However, it is your job and your responsibility to closely collaborate with your Team Leads strategically, tactically and operationally. This important aspect of being a SMART Leader becomes imperative when you or anyone in your organization have qualified concerns about a lack of leadership presence at any level.

We have found that many good managers and supervisors have fundamental shortcomings in this area. Too often, they fail to understand or accept their full responsibility for ensuring that the required leadership is present throughout the organization.

Good managers and supervisors unconsciously fail to do some or all of the following:

1. They fail to clearly articulate their leadership expectations for all three levels of organizational leadership — strategic, tactical and operational.

2. They fail to adapt their personal involvement to the level required to meet the leadership needs of the situation and the circumstance.

3. They fail to take the time to understand, appraise and provide constructive feedback regarding the leadership performance of the team leads serving in tactical and operational roles.

4. They fail to create the work environment and the internal processes required to make it non-threatening for their team leads to seek their input and involvement regarding significant leadership challenges.

5. They fail to create a culture that broadens the opportunity for all team members to develop the leadership skills and obtain the training needed to become more effective strategic, tactical and operational leaders; and

6. They fail to identify, investigate and make the decisions required to remove internal performance roadblocks.

Here is the synopsis of "Skinny" Principle #5.

SKINNY PRINCIPLE #5

Being Present with Your Presence

This Principle draws attention to the fundamental truth that without you being "present with your presence", it is nearly impossible to develop organizational cohesiveness, gain concurrence among your work teams on strategy and create the organizational momentum required to win. As your organization's leader, you must ensure that performance challenges are adequately addressed at all three levels of leadership — *strategic, tactical* and *operational.* You should also remember that you are in the only position in your organization to globally "recognize," "organize" and "sell" the improvements and changes required. It is your responsibility to focus the proper attention and to be "present with your presence" at all levels. The simplest way to think of what to keep in mind here is **"I should always make sure that I am "present" and armed with my "presence" at all levels of organizational leadership.**

THE WHAT

The "What" here is the need for managers and supervisors to create a work environment and establish the internal processes and communication channels required to make it non-threatening and comfortable for their team members —at all leadership levels — to accept and take full advantage of them being "present" and armed with their "presence".

THE WHY

"Why" is this important? We believe that there are at least two reasons that merit consideration.

The first is the fact that one of the main challenges of *leading* and *winning* within any organizational structure is finding a workable balance between giving your team leads the freedom to use their talents and you sensing when and how you must get involved — to ensure that the required leadership is "present" at all times and at all levels.

Secondly, as highlighted in this chapter's narrative, when an organization's senior leadership is "missing in action", there is a significant increase in the potential for even routine activities to "get off course" and create unforeseen organizational challenges.

THE HOW

The "How" here is two-pronged.

- "How" to assess your situation and best determine if your current work environment is one which makes it non-threatening and comfortable for your work teams, at all leadership levels, to welcome you "being present" with your presence; and

- "How" you can get moving in this direction, if it is not.

We believe that by taking the following steps, you can adequately address the fundamentals of this *"Skinny" Principle*.

STEP 1: Review the six shortcomings listed at the beginning of this chapter. Determine how many of these shortcomings you need to address and what you will do to address them. You can use the template at the end of this chapter as a guide.

STEP 2: If your organization is less than 50 team members, you should meet individually with all of your "team leads".

Here is a process you can use:

a) Share with them the type of work relationship and environment that you envision in regards to your level of involvement in the organization's tactical and operational leadership levels.

b) Then, ask for their thoughts and opinions.

c) If there is a mutual and honest consensus that such a work relationship and environment already exist, you are good.

d) If there is not such a consensus, ask for input on what he or she believes would be the best path to arrive at this type of work relationship and environment.

e) Develop a plan and implement it. The follow-up here can be included in future performance reviews.

STEP 3: If your organization is larger than 50 team members — you should meet individually with all of your "direct reports" and have a similar discussion as described in STEP 2. Then, request that all of your direct reports have and document similar discussions with their direct reports who are team leads.

THE WHEN

After you have completed an assessment of your potential "shortcomings" in this area as outlined in STEP 1, you should be in the position to determine "When" and if you should proceed to STEP 2 or STEP 3.

If you have only a couple of the shortcomings and feel confident that you have the required work environment and the relationships with all of your team members — then, that's great. However, you should consider addressing these shortcomings as soon as possible.

If you have more than a couple, you should start addressing the shortfalls immediately. Remember, if you are unknowingly *"missing in action"* there is a significant increase for the potential of even routine activities "getting off course" and creating unforeseen and unnecessary organizational challenges.

Addressing My "Being Present With My Presence" Shortcomings

Potential Shortcomings	I'M OKAY	I NEED WORK	How I Will Address This Shortcoming
1 I clearly articulate my leadership expectations for all three levels of organizational leadership —strategic, tactical and operational.			
2 I adapt my personal involvement to the level required to meet the leadership needs of the situation and circumstance.			
3 I take the time to understand, appraise and provide constructive feedback regarding the leadership performance of my team leads serving in tactical and operational roles.			
4 I create the work environment and the internal processes required to make it non-threatening for my team leads to seek my input and involvement regarding significant leadership challenges.			
5 I create a culture that broadens the opportunity for all of my team members to develop the leadership skills and obtain the training needed to become more effective strategic, tactical and operational leaders.			
6 I identify, investigate and make the decisions required to remove internal performance roadblocks.			

CHAPTER SIX

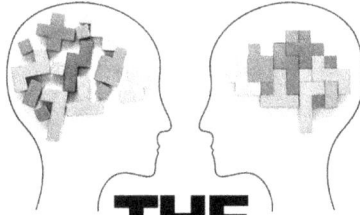

THE
SMART
LEADER
AND THE "SKINNY" PRINCIPLES

EMPATHY CAN PAY BIG DIVIDENDS

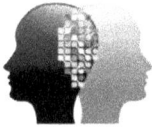

WHAT OTHERS ARE THINKING

"I think we all have empathy. We may not have enough courage to display it." — Maya Angelou

Maya Angelou
Maya Angelou was an American poet, singer, memoirist, and civil rights activist. She published seven autobiographies, three books of essays, several books of poetry, and is credited with a list of plays, movies, and television shows spanning over 50 years.

A Situational Narrative

I DIDN'T EXPECT THIS

My name is Rebecca Bushman. In January of this year, I was promoted to a Regional Vice President of Sales for Roland Pharmaceuticals. Roland Pharmaceuticals currently distributes over a thousand various pharmaceutical products to doctor offices and hospitals in the Rocky Mountain region of the United States.

Today is December 14th and there are ten business days remaining in this year. During this time of the year when most people are getting into the holiday spirit, I found myself shedding *tears of misery* and feeling a touch of depression while driving into my office this morning.

However, starting early this afternoon, I experienced a series of unexpected and welcomed events. Because of these timely events, I am now crying giant *tears of joy*.

Wow. This has been quite a journey. Through it all, I still can't believe that I was deprived of the opportunity, during my years of leadership training, to learn such a powerful *skill* and *competency*.

What were the circumstances that helped to navigate my journey and brought me to this nexus of *relief* and *disbelief* — and what is this powerful *skill* and *competency*?

****

Well. This journey began around five years ago when I started working for Roland Pharmaceuticals. I first met and became friends with the company's owners, Bob and Jennifer Roland over ten years ago.

We were all working on our MBA degrees at Denver College at the time. They both were ambitious and entrepreneurial. They talked constantly about one day owning a product distribution company.

As fate would have it, around seven years ago, Bob and Jenifer were able to purchase the assets of a bankrupt Denver-based Pharmaceutical distributor. I was so excited when I heard that Bob and Jennifer had bought the assets and had successfully launched the new entity as Roland Pharmaceuticals. Within two years of operation, they were successful in adequately capitalizing the new startup by gaining the financial support of a venture capital investment group with the exchange of 48% ownership in the company.

Not long after the investors were in place, I met Bob and Jennifer for dinner. They were still thrilled and excited. I congratulated them and inquired how things were going. During our conversation, I mentioned that I would be interested in joining the company at some point. A couple of weeks later, Jennifer called and offered me a position. I accepted the offer, left my sales management position with a major wholesale distribution company, and joined Roland Pharmaceuticals as a Senior Sales Representative.

Last year, Roland's year-over-year sales revenue increased by 43% and exceeded the $100 million mark for the first time while operating in only half of the country. It was not a secret that Roland's investment partners were interested in taking the company public via an Initial Public Offering (IPO). The goal was to raise the cash needed to expand operations nation-wide and capture some of the return on their investment.

In January of this year, as a part of the preparation for an IPO, the company appointed four new Regional Vice Presidents, including myself. We were all given a hefty number of Class B shares of Roland stock and were tasked with leading our perspective sales regions, and Roland Pharmaceuticals, to one more year of significant product sales growth. Our success would set the stage for pulling the trigger on the Roland IPO and the opportunity for the company to reward the leadership team for the long hours and hard work.

****

Now, the reason I am sitting here tonight at my desk crying big *tears of joy* instead of *tears of misery* is due to a set of attention-grabbing circumstances. Together, these circumstances would, contribute to both my success and my professional growth.

The circumstances surfaced in July of this year. This was during the part of my journey that brought me unforeseen worry and concern.

Unbelievably, almost simultaneously, all three of my top Sales Representatives, Sheniqua, Santiago and Meaghan were beset with extraordinary health, family and personal challenges.

In June of this year, my sales region was over 100% of plan. The morale and spirit of my entire sales team were through the roof. Everyone felt confident that we would meet or exceed our sales quota this year. By doing so, my region would do its part to help Roland Pharmaceuticals have another great sales year.

Since Denver was my largest metropolitan area, all three of my top Sales Representatives were in my greater Denver sales territory. It was not a surprise that the trio was responsible for over 80% of my region's product sales during the first half of the year. Each had contributed about a quarter of my region's sales through June.

It was just after the long July 4th weekend, when Sheniqua was the first of the three to approach me. She entered my office Tuesday morning profusely apologizing for having missed several sales calls at two major hospitals last week due to family problems. She later learned that her customer contacts were not incredibly happy with her right now. She inferred that she might miss her third quarter sales quota. To be totally honest, the first thing I thought was *"Well, this is what I have been afraid of since I hired her"*.

Sheniqua shared that she and her three young children had been sleeping in her van for the past few nights. She and her husband have been dealing with some irreconcilable differences in their marriage for over a year and she had finally decided to leave him and get a divorce. However, for now, she needed a few weeks off to get herself together; to find a place for her and the kids to stay; and to get back to being her old self. Having never experienced or been around any situation like this, I said, *"I am so sorry to hear this, Sheniqua. Let me think about this situation and I will get back with you tomorrow."*

Later that afternoon, Santiago's wife, Isabella, called me and shared the news that he had to be taken to the emergency room when he suddenly collapsed at home after dinner. Fortunately, it was only a mild stroke and his doctor said that he should recover fully. However, he would most likely have to miss work for at least a month. Again, my self-talk kicked in and I said to myself, *"I have always felt that he was too overweight and seemed to get too stressed out over minor things. I would have bet that he would end up in this condition."*

Having almost recovered from my conversation earlier with Sheniqua, I just took a deep breath and said, *"Isabella, I am so sorry to hear this. Glad to hear that Santiago will fully recover. Give him my best. Please let him know that I will get with him later this week, when he is better, and discuss how to manage his sales territory."*

As I was driving home that evening, wondering what else can go wrong today, my cell phone rang, and I noticed it was Meaghan calling. After I arrived home and relaxed, I listened to Meaghan's voice message.

She wanted to share that her eighty-three-year-old mother's health had taken a turn for the worst. Her mother was suffering from an advanced case of dementia and had been admitted to a memory care facility a few months ago.

Somehow, her mother was able to walk away alone from the facility this morning. Fortunately, they were able to find her a few miles down the street. Meaghan said that her mother was now safe and okay. However, since she was the only child, she had to fly down to Miami tomorrow morning to determine what she needed to do about the situation. Then she added, *"I am not sure how long I must be away from work."* I thought, *"I can really relate with Meaghan's disturbing situation. I lost my mother to the dreadful condition a few years ago and Meaghan has been such an excellent sales performer."*

After I thought about Meaghan's unfortunate circumstance for a few minutes, I returned the call to let her know that I had received her message. I told her that I was so sorry to hear the news about her mother and asked if there was anything, I could do to help. Following a lengthy conversation, I agreed to personally take over her sales calls until she was able to return to work.

Then, I suddenly began to panic a little when I realized how unthinkable it would be for me to disappoint Bob and Jennifer. I knew that, as my organization's leader, I had to make some good decisions regarding the feedback I must give Sheniqua and Santiago. More importantly, I also must craft a plan to make sure that my sales region achieves its annual sales quota.

Feeling a bit professionally overwhelmed, I made an appointment with my long-time career coach, Fred Miller. I met with Fred early the next morning over a cup of coffee.

After dumping on Fred, the details of my current dilemma and my conversations with Sheniqua, Santiago and Meaghan, he began to patiently coach me through this untravelled leadership challenge as follows:

- Fred took the time to walk me through not only *what he thought I was saying* but also *how he thought I was feeling.* I must admit that although I have worked with Fred for years, this was the first that I noticed how deeply he listened and how well he understood me.

- He shared with me that based on what he had heard — he was not concerned with me being able to handle the "management" challenges that accompanied this type of dilemma. However, he was genuinely concerned whether I would be able to generate and wrap the proper amount of *"empathy"* around all my new leadership challenges.

- Fred explained that along with the triad of challenges associated with Sheniqua, Santiago and Meaghan, a fourth new leadership challenge has also surfaced. The fourth challenge involves how I would maintain the morale and spirit of the rest of my organization — considering the possibly crippling effect of missing the top three sales reps for an extended period.

- Fred mentioned that while he was listening to the rundown of my conversation with Meaghan, he clearly sensed that I was able to be sincerely *empathetic* with her situation.

  He added, *"What I mean is that it appears that you were able to put yourself in Meaghan's shoes and completely understand her situation. Thus, you quickly made the decision on how you would treat her and her circumstance."*

- He shared that he also gathered from my conversations with Sheniqua and Santiago that, unlike Meaghan's circumstance, their similar level of concerns appeared to be totally foreign to me.

  Fred surprised me when he said, *"Not only did I sense a degree of unfamiliarity, but I also picked up on a little more than a touch of stereotyping. This is a combination which serves to make it exceedingly difficult for anyone to be* **empathetic** *and to reap the dividends to be gained from being an empathetic leader."*

- Fred managed to get and keep my undivided attention as he described the important role that a *leader's empathy* plays in developing and effectively managing workplace relationships. He walked me through how leaders lacking empathy are driven by their own needs. They also become blind or indifferent to the needs of others.

- In addition, Fred wanted to make sure that I was aware that all my other team members would be closely watching how I handled the unfortunate circumstances that have beset **Sheniqua**, **Santiago** and **Meaghan**. If they sense a genuine display of empathy from me, in handling **all three** circumstances, it will help to energize them and gain their support.

I left this unusually long, yet quite enlightening, coaching session with a plan. The primary leadership trait I would have to rely on was, without a doubt, one that was not familiar to me. However, I felt I had to trust the advice Fred had given me.

For the next five months, I studied what I should be doing as an empathic leader. I literally had to force myself to make the personal and professional changes necessary. I felt that I had no choice. I had to generate the level of empathy required to help me better understand and react to all four of my new leadership challenges — the unforeseen challenges that had just rocked my world.

I spent more time with **Sheniqua** and Santiago to get to know them better and to learn more about what it would be like to walk in their shoes. I suddenly realized how little I knew about their lives outside of the workplace. I was very unaware of the personal strengths that keeps them going daily — strengths that I had simply overlooked.

I budgeted time in my schedule to personally keep the entire team informed of how the organization was supporting **Sheniqua**, Santiago and **Meaghan** and how they were recovering from their extraordinary personal, health and family challenges.

I used weekly team-wide communications meetings and the posting of weekly performance metrics to keep everyone involved in the year-end sales push.

Consequently, I became closer to all my team members and, I found myself experiencing some of the best times I have ever had as a Sales Manager.

****

So, you see, during my drive into the office this morning, all I could think about was the $10 million dollars of revenue that my sales region needed to bring in during the ten business days remaining in the month and the fiscal year. The *tears of misery* began to flow about halfway through my drive in. That is when I finally realized how difficult it was going to be to bring in another $10 million dollars of sales this late in the year.

I was not surprised that we had gotten this close despite our poor third quarter sales performance. Once **Sheniqua**, Santiago and **Meaghan** were able to *spring back* into action and the rest of the sales team was able to exceed their prior year sales numbers during September and October, I felt we at least had a small chance to get close to reaching our goal. Historically, after the middle of December, the only year-end sales opportunities available were from customers who needed to purchase critical supplies, and these were generally small orders.

However, to my astonishment, around noon today a **series of unexpected events** began to transpire. Meaghan called a little before 1:00 PM and shared that she was able to convince two of her largest hospitals to stock up early for the coming year. This meant that she would be able to pull a new $3 million order into this fiscal year.

Around 3:00 PM Santiago called and left me a message, which stated: *"Great news Rebecca. I was able to meet with ten of my largest doctor offices last week. Together, I expect get at least $4 million of new orders. All of the orders should become additional sales and be recorded before the end of the year"*. I was so excited at this point. I literally jumped up and ran over to my manager's building to share the good news. I informed him that our chances of reaching our annual sales quota had increased significantly through the efforts of Meaghan and Santiago.

Almost breathless, I returned to my office building around 4:00 PM. To my surprise, I was told that Sheniqua was in my office waiting for me. As I walked in, she jumped to her feet with one finger in the air and said, *"Guess what Ms. B. Here it is. I got it."* Sheniqua handed me a confirmed order for $3.5 million of unplanned sales. She had spent all week, working late into the evenings to make sure that the sales are recorded this year.

As I finally caught my breathe, I began to realize that Sheniqua's additional $3.5 million of sales, combined with the $7 million of new sales reported by Meaghan and Santiago, would give us more than the $10 million dollars needed to meet our annual sales goal.

I ran over to Sheniqua and gave her a big hug, for the very first time.

****

Again, here I am. I am still sitting here in my office at the nexus of *relief* and *disbelief*. However, I am no longer mystified by why *empathy*, in the hands of an organizational leader, is such a powerful *skill* and *competency*. I am so proud of everyone for making the extraordinary effort required to *spring back* and do what was necessary to get a win here, including yours truly.

However, I must admit…*I didn't expect this*.

WHAT OTHERS ARE THINKING

"You can never understand someone unless you understand their point of view, climb in that person's skin, or stand and walk in that person's shoes." — Atticus Finch

Atticus Finch
Atticus Finch is a central character of Harper Lee's acclaimed novel *"To Kill a Mockingbird,"* published in 1960.

SKINNY PRINCIPLE #6

EMPATHY CAN PAY BIG DIVIDENDS

When most good managers and supervisors talk about leadership and being a leader, you will often hear words such as strong, strategic, passionate, confident, focused, mindful, committed and energetic.

These words are among a list of words most often used to describe leaders and leadership traits. They are also among the words that you most likely would *expect* to hear. However, have you ever heard the word *empathetic* when you hear managers and supervisors talk about leadership?

Over the years, we have learned through our experiences and the experiences of many others that, over time, *empathy* becomes one of the most important traits you must have as a leader. Empathetic leaders can better understand their team members' skill sets, their aspirations and their needs.

Think of empathy as the ability to experience and relate to the thoughts, emotions or experiences of others. Empathy is more than sympathy — which simple allows you to understand and support others with compassion or sensitivity.

For many reasons, most good managers and supervisors lack an adequate level of empathy and are not able to be empathetic when the situation demands it. Thus, they fail to reap the significant dividends that can be reaped from being a skilled, competent and *empathic* leader.

Here are the most common shortcomings we have found that can prevent the development of this critical leadership trait:

1. They fail to make the critical distinction between being *sympathetic* and being *empathetic*.

2. They fail to gain the capacity to control, express and be mindful of their own emotions. This impacts their ability to empathetically handle interpersonal relationships; and

3. They fail to be professionally thoughtful and pay attention to the "why" behind a team member's perspective, in terms of differences in gender, race, ethnicity and/or culture.

Here is the synopsis of "Skinny" Principle #6.

SKINNY PRINCIPLE #6

Empathy Can Pay Big Dividends

This Principle draws attention to the fundamental truth that being a skilled, competent and *empathetic* leader, allows you to reap significant dividends. Many of the dividends come in the form of both enhanced relationships with your team members and improved organizational performance. As an empathetic leader, you can better understand your team members as well as their skill sets, their aspirations and their needs. The simplest way to think of what to keep in mind here is **"I should remember that being empathetic with others in my organization is not the same as being sympathetic. When I am truly an empathetic leader, I feel what others are feeling. By doing so, I will come as close to reading their minds as humanly possible. Thus, I will gain hidden insights and place myself in the position to reap significant dividends for my organization and me."**

THE WHAT

The "What" here is the fundamental truth that as you progress in your role as an organizational leader and rise to new positions of authority and responsibility, you will need to sharpen your skills and your ability to be a truly empathetic leader.

The inability to be truly empathetic and to invest in getting to really know others will deprive you of the opportunity to reap significant professional and organizational dividends. Many of such dividends will come in the form of higher quality relationships; timely and meaningful decision-making insights; enhanced team member trust and commitment; as well as improved organizational performance.

THE WHY

"Why" is it important for organizational leaders to be able to listen and respond with empathy?

Here are four specific dividends that we believe can be gained by most good managers and supervisors when they work hard at being a truly empathetic leader.

1. **A More Loyal Organization**

    Retaining talented team members is one of the major challenges that every organization has to address. One of the most common reasons team members leave an organization is the lack of trust in and appreciation of the organization and its leadership. The act of empathy increases trust throughout the organization. It conveys a feeling that every team member is valued.

2. **A More Engaged Organization**

    Both *acts of empathy* and *engagement* are about feeling a connection. When your team members feel like they are cared for and their opinions and efforts matter, they naturally are more engaged and are fully absorbed by and enthusiastic about their work. By being so, they will take positive actions to further your organization's reputation and interests.

3. A More Cohesive Organization

Organizational cohesiveness is a bond that pulls team members together and works to create a productive work environment. When you demonstrate genuine empathy as the organization's leader, a culture of being professionally empathetic, caring and cohesive permeates throughout the organization.

The result can be an increase in teamwork, a decrease in conflict, and a decrease in workplace disruption. This collaboration will result in better-coordinated work effort and increased productivity.

4. A More Creative Organization

Empathy and empathetic cultures are just as important to the success of organizations as it is to individual team members. Instilling empathy in organizations can help the creative process, motivate people and create value.

Our research shows that in order to build a more creative organization you should not focus on making team members more creative. You should instead focus on creating an environment that encourages and fosters creative behaviors.

Our research also shows that the pleasure centers of the brain light up when we are empathically heard and understood. It is a nourishing connection which reduces stress and fosters resilience, trust, learning, personal growth and creativity.

THE HOW

"How" can you become an empathetic leader, if you are not one already?

Well, first, you should make the personal and professional changes required to become a genuinely *"empathetic person"*. Then, you should build an empathetic culture within your organization.

Fortunately, empathy is not a fixed trait and it can be learned. You can start your personal and professional development by finding ways to enhance your ability to sense other people's emotions. This coupled with the ability to imagine what someone else might be thinking or feeling will open new doors to developing an empathetic mindset.

One proven and frequently used method to enhance empathy skills is through professional coaching and training. Most good coaching and training sessions are geared toward helping you do much of the following:

1. Get and evaluate feedback about your relationship skills from family, friends, and colleagues.

2. Challenge yourself by undertaking difficult experiences, which push you outside of your comfort zone.

3. Explore the heart and not just the head (i.e. relationships and emotions).

4. Examine and evaluate your hidden and sometimes not-so-hidden biases.

5. Ask better and more thoughtful questions; and

6. Cultivate your sense of curiosity by asking "why" more often.

It is also possible to help change and possibly transform your current organizational culture into a more empathetic culture by simply taking some straightforward actions.

Here are a few actions you can take:

1. **Talk About Empathy**

   Let team members and superiors know that empathy matters. Explain how giving time and attention to others fosters empathy, which in turn can enhance everyone's performance and improve organizational effectiveness.

2. **Rethink How You Listen**

   To understand others and sense what they are feeling, you must be an active listener. Active listeners let others know that they are being heard, by nonverbally expressing an understanding of concerns and problems. When their leader is a good listener, team members feel respected and professional trust can develop and grow.

3. **Seek and Learn from the Perspectives of Others**

   Empathetic leaders learn and gain valuable insights by actively seeking and assessing the perspectives of others. The assessment should include taking into consideration the individual's personal experiences, gender, racial, ethnic and/or cultural differences.

THE WHEN

"When" should you start to empathize and engage?

We suggest that you began your journey today and move toward becoming a competent and empathetic leader. Empathy can pay big dividends and you should *expect* to reap them.

CHAPTER SEVEN

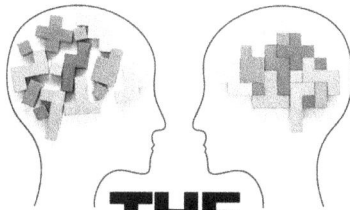

THE
SMART
LEADER
AND THE "SKINNY" PRINCIPLES

SUCCESS HAPPENS WHEN
YOU LEAVE THE ROOM

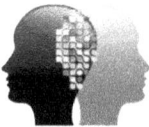

WHAT OTHERS ARE THINKING

"Become the kind of leader that people would follow voluntarily, even if you had no title or position" — Brian Tracy

Brian Tracy

Brian Tracy is a Canadian-American motivational public speaker and self-development author. He is the author of over seventy books that have been translated into dozens of languages. His popular books are *"Earn What You're Really Worth", "Eat That Frog!",* and *"The Psychology of Achievement".*

A Situational Narrative

Now, It Makes Sense

I was born at 11: 43 PM on Christmas Eve in 1967.

When I was born, my mother was six feet tall, in her late thirties and on her way to becoming a distinguished professor at a highly respected private university. My father was six feet five. He retired as the first African American Sergeant Major of the Army the same year I was born. He has since climbed the ladder to become a Commander in our state's largest police department.

As early as when I entered kindergarten, I came to grips with three of my life's realities. As it turned out, these three realities have subconsciously guided my progression through my 27-year career. They, without doubt, have also contributed greatly to the reason why I am sitting on this stage today.

The first reality is that, due to my parent's age when I was born, I soon realized that I would grow up as an only child.

The second reality is that I would always be a "girly girl" and would always enjoy competing against the boys.

The third became obvious when I inherited by grandmother's height of only about five feet four and became aware of my parent's significant professional accomplishments. Thus, I realized that I would always, literally and figuratively, be looking up to my parents.

Now, growing up in a family as the only child took its toll. One of the most challenging ordeals for me as a kid was the fact that it was nearly impossible for me to get away with anything.

However, having my parent's constant and undivided attention meant that I was able to avoid getting into any real trouble. I spent most of my time focusing on school instead of parties. Being an only child allowed me to be able to develop unique relationships with both of my parents. Most likely it would have been different if had I shared them with siblings.

Growing up as a "girly girl" allowed me to maintain interesting interpersonal and romantic relationships with the boys. But then again, I have never been afraid to tell my male classmates and coworkers that they are being sexist. My mother noticed this trait in me early in my life. She would often say *"Candi, be strong, but be fair."*

I must confess it is my relationship with both of my parents and a single piece of advice that my father gave me six years ago that is the primary reason I am sitting here today.

Just before I left Phoenix, with some hesitation, for my first and only out-of-state job opportunity, my father shared with me the following:

"Remember Candi, if you want to become the best at what you do and stand on the biggest stages; don't focus on whether or not you will be successful. Instead, for every door that opens, you should go through it focusing on mastering every aspect of the job and becoming a masterful leader — your ultimate success will depend upon what happens when you leave the room."

To be honest, I am quite nervous right now. You see, in few minutes, my name, Candace Deloris Campbell, will be called. I will then stand, walk over to the mayor, raise my right hand, and take the oath to become the first female chief of the largest police department in the state.

This means that a little girl named Candi has grown up and has earned the opportunity to be called "Chief Campbell". This will be a first in my family. As the Chief of the Phoenix Police

Department, I will lead an organization with over 2,500 sworn officers and more than 800 civilian employees along with an annual budget that exceeds $450 million.

How did I get here?

Let me first share with you a brief chronological breakdown of the "stops" along the way and "leadership growth" required of me to pull it all off. Then, I will share why my father's wise advice was so valuable and why it now makes sense.

****

In 1989, I graduated with from Arizona State University with a Bachelor of Arts degree in Public Administration and joined the Phoenix Police Department as a Patrol Officer.

Not surprising, I followed my father into a law enforcement career. When I was a freshman in high school, I told my father that my goal was to become at least a Department Commander like him. Secretly, I established a career goal of becoming the very first female Police Chief of the city of Phoenix.

My initial goal, as a Patrol Officer, was to earn the recognition of the current Police Department leadership team for being an outstanding performer. I knew that to reach the top of the leadership ranks, I would have to learn all aspects of the law enforcement profession and develop the leadership skills required to master what it takes to lead a large department.

I made a commitment to myself that would require me to treat my leadership development as seriously as all the other aspects of my professional life. I decided that at each new level of responsibility, I would *develop* and *execute* a leadership growth plan.

The plan would outline what I had to learn and how I would strategically deploy my new management and leadership skills. I also wanted to make sure that my plan included the specific actions required to develop the leadership culture I wanted to leave behind when I moved on.

In 1994, I completed graduate school with a master's degree in Education with an emphasis on leadership development and crisis management. I received the promotion to Lieutenant in October of the same year.

As a Lieutenant, I now had the responsibility for helping officers with situations that required seniority or expertise in the field. My leadership growth plan at this "stop" required me to do two things:

1. Build trust with each team member by having the courage to speak the truth on all matters; and

2. Demonstrate flexibility in my behavior.

I decided to become more flexible in my thinking and decision making by working on enhancing my personal level of emotional intelligence. I could instantly see improvement in my ability to perceive, understand and manage my emotions more accurately. I also took advantage of this newfound ability to understand the emotions of my team members. During my role as a Lieutenant, I received several internal recognitions for the level of trust that existed throughout my organizations.

In 1999, I became a Commander within the Phoenix Police Department. As a Commander, I was now responsible for overseeing day-to-day operations and personnel. This included preparing budgets; recommending personnel and capital needs; and directing or personally investigating citizen complaints about Police personnel conduct and service.

As a Commander, I was now responsible for leading a much larger organization. My leadership growth plan at this "stop" required me to do three things:

1. Maintain my organization's trust by being accountable for my team's results while helping to identify and implement solutions for improvement. I would depend on this action to encourage loyalty and excellence.

2. Work on increasing my leadership presence and influence throughout the Department. This action would help me to positively influence my team to embrace organizational goals without feeling any pressure or fear; and

3. Budget the time into my busy schedule so that I could spend some quality moments with my teams and exhibit the appropriate level of professional empathy in all situations — especially those that recognize the risk that my officers must take every day to do their jobs.

After a few months as a Commander, I noticed how my focus on being an empathetic leader was becoming contagious. I witnessed on a few occasions where my direct reports approached internal misconduct investigations in a more empathetic fashion. The culture within my organization seemed to transform into one that valued empathy coupled with responsibility.

In 2005, I received the promotion to Assistant Chief. As an Assistant Police Chief, I was responsible for assisting in the planning, directing and coordinating all activities within the Police Department.

I worked hard to get this promotion. I knew that the new role would require longer hours and would test my ability to both effectively manage and lead at the most senior levels.

The visibility I would gain throughout city government and the Phoenix community was important for me to have a chance at becoming a future Chief of Police candidate.

My leadership growth plan at this "stop" required me to do two things:

1. Exhibit a higher level of passion. This would be at a level that would send the message to everyone saying, *"I love my work. What I do inspires me and ignites my passion"*; and

2. Take every opportunity to share the Department's mission and vision statements. This includes sharing my personal interpretation of how the vision targets quality of life improvements in all the communities in Phoenix. I felt that this was a critical action to take. I felt it was important to be viewed as a visionary leader.

In 2011, I took a big and somewhat risky step in my career. I made the difficult decision to resign from the Phoenix Police Department and accept the position of the Police Chief for the City of Oxnard, California.

This was a difficult career decision for me. During the five years since becoming a Phoenix Assistant Police Chief, I had received many internal awards and public accolades. However, I had not received any indication that I was one of the top candidates to become the next Chief.

In July 2010, a friend brought to my attention the nationwide search to find a new City of Oxnard Police Chief. After a closer look, I submitted my resume of qualifications and placed myself in contention. I felt that it would at least test the strength of my resume and give me some experience in the interview process — assuming I get that far in their search.

Four months later, I had dinner with my mother and father to share with them the employment agreement I had just received to become the Police Chief for the City of Oxnard. The city of Oxnard's population was only a quarter of that of Phoenix and accordingly, the Oxnard Police Department was much smaller. There was a total of 249 sworn officers and only 129 civilians on staff.

Both my mother and father encouraged me to give the Oxnard agreement and offer serious consideration. As we were leaving dinner, my mother put her arms around me and said, *"Even though the city is smaller, you will still have the responsibility of being a Chief of Police. I know how much you have put into your many years with the*

Phoenix PD and how you will miss the strong organizations, you have helped to build. But it is a real opportunity to get some valuable experience, my dear."

With some hesitation and genuine disappointment for having to leave the Phoenix Police Department to achieve this next level of professional accomplishment, I accepted the offer and became the Police Chief for the City of Oxnard in February 2011.

I left Phoenix wondering if I would ever again get this close to becoming a Police Chief in one of the largest cities in the U.S.

Early in 2016, I learned that the City of Phoenix had recently initiated a nationwide search to find a new Police Chief.

This was really a surprise. I thought about the opportunity for a long time before I threw my hat in the ring. I had completed all the major objectives and goals I set when I joined the Oxnard Police Department as its Chief. Therefore, I was sure I would receive a good recommendation from the city of Oxnard. However, I was not sure how my performance during my many years in the Phoenix Police Department would come into play.

It is always easier to leave an organization than to return. The idea of returning as the organization's top leader, presents even more uncertainty. Nevertheless, what did I have to lose.

After, a short conversation with my parents, I made the phone call to request to be included in the search.

In October 2016, I was selected out of hundreds of applicants and a dozen candidates who were interviewed, to become the Police Chief for the City of Phoenix, the seventh largest city in the United States.

****

Now you know the "stops" and the events that are responsible for paving the way for me to be in the position to take this oath today.

So, let me get back to the advice that my father gave me six years ago and the primary reason I am sitting on this stage.

As you recall my father told me that, *"I should go through the doors of all opportunities focusing on mastering every aspect of the job and becoming a masterful leader — my ultimate success will depend upon what happens when I leave the room."*

After I was selected as the successful candidate, the chairperson of the City of Phoenix Search Committee shared with me the following.

"The strong recommendations we received from all of the teams that you led and organizations that you were a part of during your prior twenty-two years with the city of Phoenix Police Department clearly separated you from all of the other candidates. We heard many superlatives describing you and your outstanding performance as a leader. Probably the two that impressed us the most were that you were a masterful leader and that you were remarkably successful in all the positions you held."

While reflecting on this feedback, I began to realize what my father meant when he told me, *"success happens when you leave the room".*

Now, it makes sense.

SKINNY PRINCIPLE #7

SUCCESS HAPPENS WHEN
YOU LEAVE THE ROOM

O ver the many years that we have coached and lectured on the art of leading and winning, the one question we are most frequently asked is *"What would be the one thing that I could do today to become a most effective leader within my current organization?"*

Our answer has always been, *"Become a masterful leader."*

The second most frequently asked question has been *"How will I know when I have been successful as a masterful leader?"*

Our answer has always been, *"Your ultimate success will depend upon what happens when you leave the room."*

By *"become a masterful leader"*, we mean that you should become a leader who builds strong teams by first, mastering the job at hand and then building yourself a solid leadership foundation. Such a foundation will provide you with the ability and the capacity to lead others who you ask to do that job well.

For example, if the job is investing a client's money to get the best return, becoming a masterful leader first requires that you master the techniques for being successful at this trade. Then, you master how to best lead others in your organizations that are expected to be consistently successful at doing this type of work. Mastery in both cases requires knowledge, understanding, practice and the desire to do what is necessary to be among the best of those who do what you do.

When we say, *"success is what happens when you leave the room"*, we are once again referring to the fact that, as the organizational leader, your job is not to do the work. Your job is to create the environment, structure and culture for your team members to win and be successful.

When you perform your leadership role in a masterful way, those *left in the room* when you leave will perform up to and sometimes beyond the level of your expectations. Thus, *your ultimate success will depend upon what happens when you leave the room.*

Becoming a masterful leader does not require that you know everything. You should be conscious and self-aware of what you do know and acknowledge the need for your team members to fill in the blanks. On an interpersonal level, self-awareness of your strengths and weaknesses can gain the trust of others and increase your credibility.

Then again, becoming a masterful leader does require you to make a commitment to strengthen the leadership characteristics and the skills required to meet the current challenges of your organization. It also, requires that you develop and maintain an appetite for continual reflection, growth and learning.

We have found that most good managers and supervisors do have most of what it takes to become and perform as masterful leaders. However, they fail to address many of the following shortcomings that can create insurmountable roadblocks.

1. **They are reluctant to take accountability for setbacks and disappointments within their organizations**. Some even tend to place the blame on others. Masterful leaders take accountability, find solutions and encourage their team members.

2. **They routinely focus on success instead on the growth and development of their team and the work environment.** As we all know, success has many definitions and can be very challenging to achieve and

maintain. Therefore, masterful leaders focus on their team's growth and development. The goal is to ensure that their team is trained, equipped with the resources required and always in the position to win.

3. **They do not realize that their ultimate purpose within the organization is to serve**. Some managers and supervisors believe that the organization in there to serve them.

4. **They rarely reveal the appropriate level of passion about what they do**. Masterful leaders succeed because they love what they do.

Here is the synopsis of "Skinny" Principle #7.

SKINNY PRINCIPLE #7

Success Happens When You Leave the Room

This Principle draws attention to the fundamental truth that it is not what team members think, say and do while you are present and in front of them. Your ultimate success will depend upon what happens when you leave the room. This Principle emphasizes the reality that when you perform your leadership role in a masterful way, your team members will perform up to and sometimes beyond the level of your expectations in your absence. As a masterful leader, you are expected to be knowledgeable. However, you are not expected to have all of the answers. You should be conscious of what you know and acknowledge the need for your team members to fill in the blanks. The simplest way to think of what to keep in mind here is **"When I am a truly masterful leader, I can leave the room feeling that in my absence, all will be well. I should do this by being aware of what I personally bring to specific challenges while expanding the perspective and involvement of my team members to "do the work" required to win and to be successful."**

THE WHAT

The "What" here is the fundamental truth that it is not what your team members think, say and do while you are present and in front of them. It is what they think, say and do in your absence that determines the true impact that your influence, inspiration and effectiveness has on organizational performance and success.

When you perform your leadership role in a masterful way, those left in the room when you leave will perform up to and sometimes beyond the level of your expectations. Thus, your ultimate success will depend upon what happens when you leave the room.

As illustrated in this chapter's narrative, the results of Candi's leadership success during her first twenty-one years in the Phoenix Police Department didn't surface until she elected to return as Police Chief. It was through her understanding of what it would take to perform as a masterful leader and her commitment to a leadership growth plan at every "stop" along the way that propelled her ultimate success.

THE WHY

"Why" should you make the effort to do what is necessary to become and perform at the level of a masterful leader within your organization? Well, it is all about ensuring that you, your team members and your organization are consistently successful.

The success of any organization significantly depends on its leader. As Peter Drucker once said, *"Trees die from the top, so do the organizations."* When an organization has a masterful leader, it benefits from a leader who is personally effective, who has the ability to form complementary relationships with a diverse range of people and who has the ability to structure his or her team for maximum success.

THE HOW

Masterful leaders work hard at developing and maintaining a skillset that helps them achieve personal and professional success on a consistent basis. They learn how to adapt this skillset to meet the demands of the particular organization, situation or circumstance.

"How" can you become a masterful leader within your organization? We suggest that you start by taking an honest inventory of your current skillset. Then, develop a plan to obtain or strengthen the skills that are currently lacking.

To get started, you can use the *"Masterful Leader Skills Inventory Checklist"* at the end of this chapter. The checklist focuses on the four main areas of mastery required to be successful within any organizational structure: They are:

- Personal Effectiveness.
- Relationship Engagement.
- Team Building & Development; and
- Leadership Influence.

Remember, mastery requires deliberate practice. Here are seven keys to deliberate practice:

1. Establish well-defined and specific goals.

2. Develop a practice plan and stick to it.

3. Break your tasks down into parts.

4. Give each part your full attention.

5. Get feedback from someone who has mastered your current role.

6. Move out of your comfort zone; and

7. Maintain your motivation --- motivation is mastery's fuel.

THE WHEN

"When" should you get started with this key leadership transformation? We suggest you get started only when you have made a commitment to allocate the personal time and to acquire the developmental resources required to successfully complete the transformation from good manager or supervisor to masterful leader.

Remember, as a masterful leader, you will:

- ✓ Stay true to your vision.
- ✓ Practice humility.
- ✓ Leave your ego at the door when you enter a room; and
- ✓ Feel that all will be well when you leave the room.

Masterful Leader Skills Inventory Checklist

Personal Effectiveness	YES	NO
I am confident and composed under pressure.		
I have excellence in judgement, critical thinking and decision-making.		
I have the ability to create better, easier, more efficient results, by optimizing my resources.		
I have the capability to solve complex problems and create effective strategies.		

Relationship Engagement	YES	NO
I have the ability to form complementary relationships with a diverse range of people.		
I have the ability to have positive engagements with people regardless of how difficult they may be at times.		
I have the ability to effectively solve conflict and create mutually beneficial solutions.		
I have the ability to understand, work with, and influence colleagues.		

Team Building & Development	YES	NO
I have the ability to structure my work teams for maximum effectiveness.		
I am capable of understanding how to develop a cohesive sense of team.		
I have the ability to identify areas for development in order to create high performance.		
I have the confidence and ability to establish effective teamwork through cohesive systems.		

Leadership Influence	YES	NO
I have the ability to envision outcomes and formulate an effective plan.		
I have the ability, capacity and courage to communicate with influence.		
I am capable of solving complex problems and creating effective solutions.		
I have the ability to adapt, inspire, direct and organize the efforts of the people who follow my lead.		

WHAT OTHERS ARE THINKING

"Success lies in a masterful consistency around the fundamentals."
—— Robin S. Sharma

Robin S. Sharma

Robin Sharma is one of the world's premier speakers on Leadership and Personal Mastery, recently named one of the World's Top Leadership Gurus.

CHAPTER EIGHT

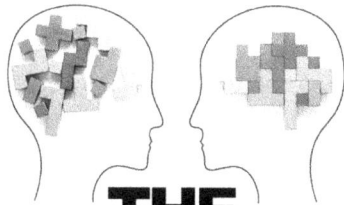

THE
SMART
LEADER
AND THE "SKINNY" PRINCIPLES

WINNING THE BATTLES DOESN'T ALWAYS WIN THE WAR

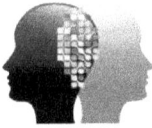

WHAT OTHERS ARE THINKING

"The general who wins the battle makes many calculations in his temple before the battle is fought. The general who loses makes but few calculations beforehand." – Sun Tzu

Sun Tzu

Sun Tzu is an enigma - his birth and death dates are unknown; he may or may not have written the book for which he is famous; and his very historicity remains in question. He is credited with writing *"The Art of Work"*, a well-crafted guide to strategy in battle.

A Situational Narrative

THE TREES GOT ME

My name is Frances Rodriguez.

Twenty-four hours ago, I was the Lead Supervisor of the Flight Information System and Training Department for Miracle Mile Aerospace. I am now sitting at my desk in my home office, working on an updated resume while goggling "goals", "strategy" and "tactics". As I have recently and painfully learned, it's never too late to make sure you have a firm grasp of the fundamentals.

If this doesn't make sense to you, you're not alone.

Here's a little background on a dreadful situation. In hindsight, it is a situation I could have avoided by simply realizing that, even within organizations, winning the battles doesn't always win the war.

Over the past five months, I have spent six days a week and ten hours a day leading a major company initiative. At the outset, I was convinced that this effort would lead to accolades for my team and a promotion for me. Instead, I was removed from my Department Supervisor's position two weeks ago. Then I was dismissed from the company yesterday morning. The reasons given were *"your inability to perform at the required level and your failure to maintain internal safety practices."*

I still believe that my firing was due more to the political pressure that Miracle Mile was receiving because of the two recent airplane mishaps, but I will never really know. Fortunately, no lives were lost. What I do know is that up until it all "hit the fan" two weeks ago, I sincerely believed I was winning the battles and doing exactly what was expected of me.

During my exit interview yesterday, Gloria Hawkins, the Director of Human Resources, agreed that the company's strategy for implementing the initiative may not have been clearly articulated during the later stages of its rollout. In her words, *"Jimmy John, the Chief Operating Officer, could have done a better job communicating the fundamental challenges associated with the initiative's financial success and the need to maintain operational safety."* Then she added, *"However Frances, it has to be assumed that someone at your level of responsibility should have been able to understand these fundamentals and certainly not risk the possibility of a major safety mishap.*

Now, here is what I did, what I didn't do and what I learned.

****

What I did.

This new initiative was code-named, "Safety And More Profits" or SAMP for short. I was aware that versions of the SAMP initiative had been launched successfully in three other departments prior to being launched in my Flight Information System and Training (FISAT) Department in June of this year. Everyone talked about how the Supervisors of those three departments quickly received grade promotions because of their success.

In a meeting with the COO during the initiative kick-off, I learned that FISAT would be the last department to launch SAMP this fiscal year. All three of the prior departments were responsible for a variety of flight control hardware upgrades. As a part of the SAMP initiative, certain "safety upgrades" were to now be sold as "optional" safety features on new airplanes and "upgrade options" to existing airlines currently flying Miracle Mile aircraft.

I heard through the grapevine that all three of the prior departments had met or exceeded the anticipated financial targets for "safety option" sales. The metric used to determine their "success" was documented in a new company report titled, *New Safety Options Sales Strategy and Guidelines.*

Unfortunately, I didn't receive a copy of the new report. I did make a note to myself to review a copy. But, of course, I never got around to reviewing a copy and gaining more insight into the initiative's rollout strategy. Based on my twenty-five years of experience, I felt comfortable with my vision of how to proceed and be successful in launching SAMP within my department.

After attending several additional meetings with the COO, I surmised that if the SAMP rollout was also successful in my department, it would help Miracle Mile meet its overall financial goal for the fiscal year. I also assumed it would help me get the expected grade promotion.

So, based on what I knew at this point about the initiative, I established the goals, implementation strategy and operational tactics we would use to successfully launch SAMP within my organization.

The primary goal was to identify as many opportunities to rollback once "standard" safety documentation features as possible. These features would then be sold as "safety options" going forward.

My strategy was to have our sales team use recent "feature use data history" to support why the features are now considered optional to existing customers. Then, we would offer the safety features as options on all new Miracle Mile aircraft. In addition, I decided to offer a special discount on "safety option" sales to existing airlines currently operating without the safety features.

I spent hours devising the operational tactics to ensure that we met the anticipated sales goal for our "safety options" this fiscal year.

In an all-hands meeting, I instructed my team to increase the number of safety feature option sales by first, systematically contacting all the airlines operating Miracle Mile planes and discussing airplane safety. Then, using a written script that I had developed, they were to make a *hard sales push* and persuade the airline to purchase the optional safety documentation for their existing flight information systems.

The internal battles started when a few of my team leads began to express concerns regarding the lack of certain pilot navigation documentation on Miracle Mile planes flying into airports with short runways. They suggested several different approaches to rolling out the SAMP initiative in our department. Some of their suggestions even involved taking pilot surveys and waiting for pilot feedback.

Because most of what the team suggested would extend the SAMP initiative rollout beyond the end of the fiscal year, I overruled the suggestions and eventually won all these battles by forcefully instructing everyone to move full speed ahead.

Up until two weeks ago, it appeared that we were being successful by exceeding the number of anticipated customer contacts and "safety option" sales. Then, it all "hit the fan".

Two airlines flying new Miracle Mile planes out of small airports were forced to make emergency landings. One incident involved a near mid-air collision with another plane preparing to land. The forced landings were caused by a navigation alert that was traced back to a latent hardware defect in a pilot control assist device. The device could have been easily overridden in flight, if the pilots of those planes had the safety documentation required in their flight information system. The documentation in question was, of course, a part of the safety documentation that my department had offered to both airlines only as a "safety option".

****

What I didn't do.

As I sit here today and reflect on the past five months, I can now see clearly what went wrong.

Without any doubt, I worked hard on planning and leading every aspect of the SAMP initiative rollout in my department. I spent a lot of time thinking through the details and making what I thought were good assumptions about what was being asked of me and what was required for me and my team to be successful.

However, in hindsight, it was not what I did, but what I didn't do that caused this dreadful situation. Here is what I didn't do and what would have made a difference in the outcome.

1. I didn't realize that my role as Lead Supervisor required me to make sure that I clearly understood my company's top-level strategies and to determine how to incorporate them into what my organization was being asked to do.

   My failure to read the company's report on the SAMP initiative, denied me the opportunity to "see the big picture". If I had read the report, I would have been aware that it strongly emphasized the following, *"A key component of a successful SAMP initiative implementation strategy is for all department leaders to be extremely mindful of NOT sacrificing aircraft operational safety. Remember, operational safety trumps option sales."*

2. I didn't listen to my team leads when they expressed concerns about the potential flight safety of some aircraft. Instead, I remained in the "bowels" of the initiative's implementation. By doing so, I considered my experts' feedback, as "competition" to my plans. Unfortunately, I lost sight of the "war" and made sure that I would win all of the "battles".

3. In my meeting with my senior management, I didn't have the wherewithal and the courage to directly ask some

important questions about the company's SAMP initiative rollout strategy and flight safety concerns within my department.

I should have made sure that the COO was aware of the unique challenges associated with selecting and selling "safety options" in flight information systems versus other types of system upgrades. I should have known that, as the most knowledgeable person in the room on this topic, I was expected to provide leadership in this area.

4. I failed to gather the level of emotional intelligence needed at the time to effectively lead my team. I should not have allowed the possibility of "accolades for my team and a promotion for me" to overshadow the clarity of my thinking, planning and motivation. In hindsight, I now see that all my plans, goals, strategy and tactics targeted "option sales" and not flight safety.

    As Gloria Hawkins, the Director of Human Resources, pointed out, *"someone at my level of responsibility should have been able to understand these fundamentals."*

****

What I learned.

I must admit that I am embarrassed about what I learned or should I say, "once again learned".

Even though I am aware of the need to think and plan based on sound "goals", "strategy" and "tactics", I was reminded that leaders must also approach the development of goals, strategy and tactics with a focus on the "forest" and not the "trees".

Simply put, in this case, *the trees got me.*

SKINNY PRINCIPLE #8

WINNING THE BATTLES
DOESN'T ALWAYS WIN THE WAR

Yes. The rush associated with winning has a way of making all of us feel that we are on top of the world. However, as the organization's leader, you have the responsibility to make sure that the battles your teams are winning are the battles that will lead to achieving your organization's overarching goals.

We have learned that this is one area of leadership competency where most good supervisors and managers tend to struggle. The struggle is both foundational and emotional. On the foundational level, the struggle involves the inability to "mentally model" what leadership focus to give specific situations. Most managers and supervisors often mimic behaviors learned from observing other leaders. The ability to prudently establish goals and strategies that are consistent with overarching corporate goals requires the effective use of three key foundational leadership skills: Conflict Resolution, Effective Communications and Influence.

On the emotional level, the struggle involves the lack of adequate growth in the emotional intelligence required to resolve potential conflicts. Of course, emotional intelligence is the ability to effectively manage your own feelings so that negative feelings don't overwhelm or affect sound judgment and decision-making. This would include the emotions surrounding your desires, expectations, beliefs, prejudices and fears.

Why do most good supervisors and managers tend to continue to struggle is this area? Here are the most difficult hurdles.

1. **Winning the battle of conflict avoidance.** Conflict avoidance is prevalent within all organizational structures. Even among good managers and supervisors, there is a natural tendency to rationalize the need to confront conflict.

2. **Organizational and operational inconsistencies.** Most inconsistencies within organizations are usually the result of organizational and leadership misalignment.

   Unfortunately, neither cures itself naturally. Resolution requires sincere intervention and honesty at all levels.

3. **Sufficient growth in emotional intelligence.** Unlike the Intelligence Quotient (IQ), Emotional Intelligence (EQ) does not change significantly over our lifetime. However, EQ can evolve with a desire to learn and grow.

Here is the synopsis of "Skinny" Principle #8.

SKINNY PRINCIPLE #8

Winning the Battles Doesn't Always Win the War

This Principle draws attention to the fundamental truth that, as the leader, you have the responsibility for making sure that the battles your teams are winning are the battles that will lead to achieving your organization's overarching goals. If there is ever any doubt concerning how your team's goals, strategies and tactics stack up against those at the corporate level, you must have the wherewithal and courage to address the conflict head-on. Effective leaders know that it is their responsibility to recognize the conflict and to work at all levels of the organization. The simplest way to think of what to keep in mind here is **I must remember that, as my organization's leader, my primary leadership focus should always be on the *forest* and not the *trees*.**

THE WHAT

The "What" here is the need to fortify your ability to win and lead by initially focusing on the broadest objective (i.e. the forest) and not just the operational details (i.e. the trees) during the planning process of a new organizational initiative or project.

We are sure that you would agree that successful outcomes start with good plan. All good plans consist of the right goals; the right strategies to achieve those goals; and the right tactics to successfully implement those strategies. In addition, winning the battles in the trenches is always necessary to achieve positive and successful outcomes. One of your primary responsibilities, as the organization's leader, is to make sure that the battles fought contribute to winning the the organization's ultimate goals and objectives.

The best way to do this is by establishing plans that are consistent with overarching corporate goals. By doing so, you will eliminate *dreadful situations* similar to the one that Frances, in this chapter's narrative, found herself reflecting upon.

THE WHY

There are many reasons "Why" fortifying your ability to lead and win the unavoidable battles is important. However, failing to make sure that the battles your teams are winning are the "right" battles can lead to disastrous and unrecoverable situations.

Most good managers and supervisors struggle to successfully navigate in this area and many find themselves in difficult and unnecessary circumstances. Therefore, developing and perfecting your leadership competency in this area should be a priority.

You should add to your self-awareness routine the time to monitor any foundational and emotional shortcomings in this area and eliminate them by taking specific developmental actions.

THE HOW

"How" to fortify foundational and emotional shortcomings in this area will vary based on your personal genealogical, psychological and motivational traits. However, we suggest that you "test drive" some of the following techniques for addressing the three specific hurdles discussed earlier in this chapter.

1. **Conflict Avoidance**

    ▪ **Express your contrary opinion as an "and."**

    Keep in mind that it is not necessary for someone else to be wrong for you to be right.

    ▪ **Use hypotheticals.**

    If you don't feel absolutely comfortable being assertive when addressing a co-worker or superior, then ask them to imagine a different scenario.

    ▪ **Discuss the perceived impact of the action.**

    Instead of simply disagreeing with the action, help others think through the consequences by asking good open-ended questions about the potential impact.

    ▪ **Ask about the underlying issue.**

    If you disagree, start the discussion by making an attempt to clarify and understand the other person's rationale. If you understand the reason for the action, you might be able to mutually find another way to accomplish the same goal.

2. **Leadership Deficiencies and Misalignments**

    ▪ **Consider establishing alignment on the "why".**

    Some senior leaders spend a significant about of time communicating the "what" and the "how". Encourage discussions on the "why" to gain a better appreciation and to learn how to better establish lower-level goals, strategies and tactics that are aligned with broader objectives.

- **Mutually define what winning looks like.**

  Envisioning what winning looks like at all levels within the organization is a critical part of achieving the broader success.

- **Set regular check-ins to stay aligned.**

  Regularly scheduled meetings and communication sessions at all levels of the organization is vital to staying aligned. Year-to-year priorities do shift. Effective leaders must be prepared and ready to adapt.

3. Evolving Your Emotional Intelligence

- **Find comfortable ways to maintain a positive attitude.**

  Emotionally intelligent leaders have an awareness of the moods of those around them and guard their attitude accordingly.

- **Become more approachable and sociable.**

  Emotionally intelligent leaders maintain a smile and a positive presence.

- **Respond rather than react to conflict.**

  Conflict can naturally cause emotional and regrettable outbursts as well as feelings of anger. The emotionally intelligent leader stays calm during stressful situations.

- **Show your passion and motivation.**

  Emotionally intelligent leaders are self-motivated. Their attitude and passion motivates others. Their passion inspires passion in others, builds trust and allows for more comfortable conversations surrounding conflicts.

- **Learn how to take criticism with a balanced mindset.**

    Instead of getting offended or self-protective, take a few moments to understand the basis of the critique and how to constructively resolve the concerns.

- **Develop a positive yet assertive communications style.**

    Positive and assertive communication can help to earn respect without coming across as aggressive or passive. Emotionally intelligent leaders understand this and know how to communicate their opinions and needs in a direct way while still respecting others.

THE WHEN

"When" you have determined what works best, you should consciously, methodically and routinely integrate these techniques into your growing "tool kit" of leadership fundamentals.

Remember, you should always make an extra effort to ensure that *"the trees don't get you"*.

CHAPTER NINE

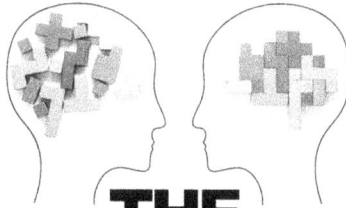

THE
SMART
LEADER
AND THE "SKINNY" PRINCIPLES

INSPIRING MUTUAL TRUST IS JOB ONE

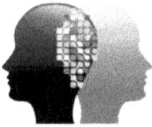

WHAT OTHERS ARE THINKING

"Leadership without mutual trust is a contradiction in terms."
—— Warren Bennis

Warren Bennis

Warren Bennis was an American scholar, organizational consultant and author, widely regarded as a pioneer of the contemporary field of Leadership studies. He was University Professor and Distinguished Professor of Business Administration and Founding Chairman of The Leadership Institute at the University of Southern California.

A Situational Narrative

I ONLY NEEDED TO BE LIKE MIKE

It was a *very close call.*

However, Charlie Yang is still the President and CEO of the Better Way Foundation. As the CEO, he oversees the National Office and all Branch Operations.

I am a long-time member of the Better Way Foundation Board of Directors. I was the Chairman of the Board eight year ago when Charlie was selected after a national search to become only the second President of the twenty-five-year-old organization.

The Founding President and CEO, Michael (Mike) Monahan, lost his fight with cancer a little more than a year earlier. Mike founded the Better Way Foundation when he was only 24 years old. Over the years, Mike became a trusted leader and was greatly admired by the entire organization.

Let me first share a little history of the organization.

Then, I will explain why it was such a close call for Charlie to retain his job, secure a new four-year employment agreement and, more importantly, regain the trust of the organization that once viewed him as the "second coming of Mike".

The first branch of the Better Way Foundation was founded in 1974 as a community-based, non-profit organization. The multi-million-dollar organization currently has seventy-four local Branch Offices located throughout the United States.

The Better Way promotes and supports the common good in small communities with a focus on education, income and health—the building blocks for a better way of life.

Each Better Way Branch Office has a Director, a small staff and a local Advisory Board selected from highly respected members of the community. The National Office of the foundation manages the operational performance and governance of all Branch Offices. Each Branch works closely with the National Office and administers all local programs and initiatives.

This quasi-decentralized management and leadership approach has achieved national acclaim. The approach is considered the primary reason the non-profit has been able to expand so rapidly and garner so much success in accomplishing its mission.

With the rapid growth of new Branch Offices, the founding President made it a priority in his work schedule to visit each Branch at least every other month. Mike often shared, with anyone who would listen, his leadership motto. The motto was even on the back of his business card and read, *"Listen First, Talk Straight, Right Wrongs and Extend Trust."*

Everyone was aware of Mike's leadership style and preparation. Prior to each Branch visit, he would make sure that he was knowledgeable of the Branch's ongoing activities and unique challenges. His visits always included time for him to personally establish, grow, extend and, if needed, restore trust with Branch Directors and their staff.

During his meetings, Mike would stress the need for each Branch Director to inspire and maintain a high level of trust and credibility. These face-to-face coaching sessions revealed Mike's passion and motivated the Branch Directors to eagerly follow his lead. At times, he would privately share with me that the, near weekly, trips were physically exhausting but as he would put it, *"inspiring and maintaining mutual trust should be job one for anyone who leads any type of organization."*

144

****

Immediately after assuming the role of the Better Way's President, Charlie visited each of the Branch Offices and met with the Directors. He made sure, that before he ended the visit, he would ask each Director the same question, *"What do you expect of me as the new Better Way President and CEO?"*

In all cases, his notes would reflect the same answer, *"you should be like Mike."*

During the first four years as President, Charlie met all the Board's expectations. He followed the advice of his Branch Directors. He was very much *"like Mike"* and the performance of the organization didn't miss a beat. As the result of his winning performance, the board offered Charlie a second four-year employment agreement.

****

Now, as I understand it, about six months after signing the new employment agreement, Charlie hired the services of a well-known executive coaching firm. He was apparently growing tired of the extensive travel. He was also concerned about the increasing cost of operations. Charlie felt he needed some advice on how he could modify the current organizational leadership approach. The goal was to make the entire organization less dependent on his presence and more cost efficient.

After spending about three months working with his coach to develop a plan, Charlie announced the National Office's new leadership strategy and organizational changes.

The announcement was communicated to all seventy-four Branch Directors in the form of a series of three mass emails.

The first email detailed the reasoning for the need to modify the Better Way's leadership approach. In the same email, he revealed his new leadership motto, *"Decentralize, Reduce Operational Cost and Grow Foundation Reserves."*

The second email announced the change of his personal Branch visits from bi-monthly to once a year. It also announced the establishment of a new monthly Branch Conference Call. The call would include all Better Way Branch Directors and would be limited to one hour. The National Office would develop the agenda based on what it perceived as the month's top priorities.

The third email announced a proposal he was preparing to submit to the Better Way Foundation Board of Directors within a few months. He was proposing the closure of at least twenty-five Branch Offices over the next three years.

****

The announcement and the abrupt changes were a real shock to the entire organization. The other members the Better Way Board of Directors first learned of Charlie's organizational changes when I forwarded them the emails that one of the Branch Directors shared with me following a long and surprising phone conversation.

****

What occurred over the next three and a half years within the Better Way organization can best be described as *"a chaotic and predicable performance melt down"*.

Here is a brief summation of the major occurrences.

- The Better Way Board of Directors was disappointed that they didn't receive a briefing on the plan and the announcement prior to its release. They also felt that Charlie should have chosen a more personal method to announce such a major organizational change.

- However, to support Charlie and give his new plan a chance, the Better Way Board agreed with the idea of closing some Branch offices. As anticipated, this part of the announcement created a high degree of discomfort among the Branch Directors and their staff.

- During the first few months of the Branch Conference Call, the Branch Directors asked dozens of questions in the hope of clarifying the confusion surrounding the new decentralized Branch Office operating approach. Charlie indicated that he would get back with them. However, and unfortunately, he rarely did.

- It didn't take long for the monthly conference call to turn into a monologue. Charlie would share his concerns regarding Branch performance issues and the Branch Directors soon learned to simply, just listen.

- The lack of clear direction from the National Office and unreliable responses to their questions forced the Branch Directors to go it alone and to implement inconsistent local operating procedures.

- Charlie soon noticed that during his annual Branch Office visits, the meetings with the Directors and staff began to get shorter and more formal. Once casual, open and candid discussions were now rehearsed PowerPoint presentations.

- The monthly Branch Conference Call quickly morphed into heated discussions about methods to reduce Branch Office overhead cost, to better utilize local office staff and to improve Branch cost performance.

- Two years after launching the changes, no Branch Offices were closed, and the Foundation's overhead cost had increased by more than 40%. It was also becoming more difficult for the National Office to get detailed financial information and operating performance measures from the Branch Offices.

- For the first time in its history, the Better Way Foundation established and hired a staff of internal auditors. The National Office assigned an auditor to each

Branch Office. The new Group of seventy-four auditors reported directly to Charlie.

- Because the cost for the new Audit Group was higher than what Charlie anticipated, he directed that the Group's annual cost be charged back to the Branch Offices without any increase in Branch overhead budgets.

- In January of the final year of Charlie Yang's second employment agreement, the Better Way Foundation Board initiated an organization-wide Employee Attitude Survey. The Board of Directors' Management & Compensation Committee was required to conduct the survey. It was a part of the normal process for either extending or drafting a new employment agreement for the President and Chief Executive Officer position.

- The results of the survey were presented to the Board of Directors during a special meeting in May. Charlie was not invited to the meeting and he was not present.

- The Survey consultants presented the following Executive Summary of the recent findings:

    1. The morale throughout the organization is at the lowest level recorded during the five times this attitude survey has been conducted within the Better Way organization over the past twenty-one years.

    2. The top five responses listed as the potential causes for the drop in morale were:

        ✓ The lack of honest communications between the National Office and the Branch Directors.

        ✓ The lack of clear direction and support from the National Office.

        ✓ The lack of respect and appreciation of the work performed at the Branch level.

- ✓ The National Office's failure to keep key commitments made to the Branch Offices; and

- ✓ The loss of trust at all levels of the organization and in its leadership.

3. When asked, *"What would be the one change you would like to see in the organization at this time"*, 96% of the employee respondents said, *"a change in leadership at the top"*.

****

As the Chair of the Board's Management & Compensation Committee, I was tasked with developing the Board's approach to addressing the concerns expressed in the recent Employee Attitude Survey. I was also asked to meet with Charlie Yang, share with him the survey results and determine if the Better Way should express any interest in retaining Charlie's services as the Better Way President and CEO beyond his current agreement.

I met with Charlie two weeks later over a cup of coffee. He had a week to review his copy of the Employee Attitude Survey responses and the Executive Summary presented to the Board of Directors.

When Charlie entered the café, I could see the look of grave disappointment on his face. As soon as he sat down, he began to apologize for the direction that he had taken the organization. He agreed 100% that the buck stopped at his office.

In his words, *"I know that my miserable performance as the Better Way President over the last three years does not deserve an extension of the current or a new employment agreement."*

I could tell that he had lost all the confidence and trust he once had in his ability to lead the organization. Having held many senior leadership roles in large organizations during my career, instead of diving into what he did wrong, I spelled out the three things he had to do over the next six months to retain his job.

They were:

1. First, you must regain the confidence and trust needed in yourself to continue in a senior leadership role.

2. Secondly, you must rebuild the trust within the Better Way organization back to the levels you found when you arrived, almost eight years ago; and

3. Lastly, you must make a presentation to the full Board of Directors during the December Board meeting. We all would like to hear at that time why you believe you should be retained as the Better Way President and CEO.

****

When Charlie entered the meeting room that evening in December, I don't believe any of the Board members felt he had any chance of retaining his job.

Charlie confidently opened his presentation by admitting to the Board that he had "masterfully screwed up" and should not have made major changes in the Better Way's leadership approach and operational strategy. In his words, *"I had convinced myself that the success I experienced during my first four years as the Better Way's President was all about me. I completely ignored the foundation that Mike Monahan had spent decades building to create this great organization."*

Charlie went on to provide the Board a recap of how he had spent the past six months. He had met for days with each Branch Director and their staff members. He admitted his "screw-up" to them and accepted all the blame. He also sincerely asked the Branch Directors for their candid and honest feedback.

In a remorseful voice, Charlie added, *"More importantly, for the first time I really listened. I made a commitment to involve all the Directors in a plan to right the wrongs—and it's a commitment I plan to keep. The goal will be to rebuild trust within the Better Way team and for us to return to being the strong organization we once were."*

Then, slowly Charlie walked over to the Board Chair and handed her a large envelope. Inside the envelope was a thick document. It was a ninety-five-page plan outlining the specific steps that he and his Branch Directors have agreed to take over the next twelve months to achieve the goal.

At the back of the document were the signatures of all seventy-four local Branch Directors.

****

Charlie and I met for dinner around the middle of January. We both had experienced delightful and enjoyable holiday seasons. We swapped stories about the holiday parties attended and the gifts we had received.

Although the 5 to 4 vote of approval by the Board of Directors was a *very close call*, Charlie also received a special gift earlier this month—a new four-year employment contract to continue as the Better Way's President and CEO.

I congratulated him for stepping up to the plate and doing what was "needed" to right the wrongs. Charlie smiled, and said, *"I could shoot myself for not seeing the writing on the wall four years ago."*

When I asked Charlie what he was suggesting, he quickly replied, *"I only needed to be like Mike."*

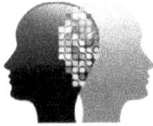

WHAT OTHERS ARE THINKING

"Trust starts with trustworthy leadership. It must be built into the corporate culture" — Barbara Brooks Kimmel

Barbara Brooks Kimmel

Barbara Brooks Kimmel is Co-founder and Executive Director of Trust Across America -Trust Around the World and editor of Trust Inc. Strategies for Building Your Company's Most Valuable Asset. In 2012 Barbara was named one of "25 Women who are Changing the World" by Good Business International.

SKINNY PRINCIPLE #9

INSPIRING MUTUAL TRUST IS JOB ONE

O ne of the most important jobs of any leader is to inspire and maintain a culture of trust throughout the organization.

Many global studies have shown that organizations that operate with a high level of trust among its leaders and team members have increased productivity, improved morale and the ability to work more effectively.

We have learned that just as the presence of high trust within an organization has great benefits, the lack of trust within an organization can carry a significant cost. When trust is low, within an organization, there is often a "hidden cost" attached to all decisions, interactions, transactions, communications, and other actions required to get the job done. The cost is associated with longer discussions, more questions and extended approval cycles.

However, sometimes, the additional cost is not hidden and is quite visible—such as the addition of more internal controls and auditors similar to the action taken by Charlie Yang in this chapter's narrative. Because of the lost of trust, Charlie felt that he needed to gain more insight into what was really happening at the lower levels of the Better Way Foundation. In his efforts to "reduce cost", he was adding hidden cost and inefficiency to his organization.

Unfortunately, for many good managers and supervisors, the real challenge is figuring out how to "regain" or strengthen trust in existing organizational relationships.

153

How do most leaders find themselves in this position? Well, here are a few of the actions that can be taken to inspire and maintain trust that they fail to embrace:

1. They too often, fail to align their words and actions.

2. They fail to admit their mistakes yet are quick to call out the mistakes of others.

3. They fail to accept the blame when their organizations fall short of expectations.

4. They fail to ensure that all their communication is clear, concise and thoughtful; and

5. They repeatedly fail to simply be truthful and honest when responding to difficult or challenges situations.

Here is the synopsis of "Skinny" Principle #9.

SKINNY PRINCIPLE #9
Inspiring Mutual Trust is Job One

This Principle draws attention to the fundamental truth that as your organization's leader, you should make it a priority to develop and maintain the ability to establish, grow and re-build trust throughout your organization. Trust is an intellectual asset, a skill and an influencing power. However, trust is complex because it is intangible. Trust can be earned with competence, integrity, benevolence and credibility. Trust can be lost by being perceived as inauthentic, making false promises or lacking clarity in communications. When a team has trust in their leader, it improves communication, increases creativity and enhances productivity. The simplest way to think of what to keep in mind here is **"As a leader, I should never forget that it is the trustworthiness of my actions and behavior that matters most to my team and my organization."**

THE WHAT

The "What" here is that, as your organization's leader, you should make it a priority to develop and maintain the ability to establish, grow and extend trust throughout your organization.

THE WHY

Trust in the workplace is a fundamental building block of any organization. Not only does the lack of trust add inefficiency and cost, issues pertaining to trust are some of the most difficult challenges that can surface within any organizational structure.

As we noticed in this chapter's narrative, issues pertaining to the loss of trust can destroy an organization's culture. When your team members perceive you as trustworthy, they have confidence in you, in your integrity and in your ability to lead them to victory.

THE HOW

"How" should you, as your organization's leader, perceive the trust you have worked hard to earn from your team members, co-workers and superiors? Well, the bottom line is that none of them would give their thoughts, passion, loyalty and best effort to anyone they didn't trust. So, you should think of the "trust" that your organization has in you as your "workplace currency". This is a currency you must use every day to carry out your leadership role and to achieve organizational goals.

However, there is also a second and third "How" in this area. They are:

1. "How" to establish and grow trust throughout your organization; and

2. "How" to regain trust that has been lost.

How to Establish and Grow Trust

The issue of trust in the workplace can make or break an organization's culture. If you don't cultivate the kind of trust that creates enjoyment, unity and productivity, then your organization will slowly and steadily weaken from within.

We define trust as your organization's willingness to be open and honest, based on the belief that another individual, team, or group is also competent, open, honest, reliable, and identify with common organizational goals.

Therefore, as your organization's leader, establishing and growing trust should be one of your primary priorities. Here are some pointers that you should keep in mind.

1. **You should recognize that building trust takes hard work.**

    Trust must be earned. Another person's trust is based on your conscious effort to "walk your talk" and keep your promises to everyone with whom you interact.

2. **You should be honest and supportive.**

    You should always tell the truth, even in difficult situations. Don't get into the habit of just saying what you think people want to hear. Being supportive of your team members and co-workers can go a long way toward building trust as a leader.

3. **Commit to follow through.**

    Even the best messages you communicate will be muted if you don't follow through with corresponding action. Not following through on commitments can easily destroy your hard-earned trust.

4. **Be consistent.**

    When you consistently do what you say, you will build trust over time. Keeping commitments must be the essence of your behavior, in all relationships, day after day and year after year.

5. Model the behavior you seek.

Nothing speaks louder about the culture of your organization than your behavior as the leader. Your behavior influences team member actions and drives their results.

6. Build in accountability.

When you acknowledge your mistakes as well as successes, team members perceive you as being trustworthy.

How to Regain Trust That Has Been Lost

Of all the things in the world to try to recover, lost trust proves to be one of the most difficult. You can rebuild trust within your team and organization, over time, by taking positive and sincere actions. Here are some suggestions.

1. Start With Yourself

You should take personal accountability for restoring trust. This is versus waiting for others to come to their senses and change their behavior. To expect your team members and co-workers to instantly trust you again is unreasonable and will only continue to undermine their trust in your leadership.

2. Engage In "Difficult Conversations"

When trust breaks down within an organization, often communication also breaks down and becomes more difficult. As your organization's leader who has taken accountability for regaining trust, you must have the courage to have the uncomfortable conversations. You can start the process by stating the obvious (i.e. there is a lack of trust). Then you should clearly express your intention to re-establish trust.

3. Listen With Empathy

You should acknowledge the disappointment, anger or hurt feelings on all sides that are associated with the lost trust. You should resist defending your prior actions. Instead, you should find common goals that look to the future. You should agree on how you will give each other feedback on the agreed upon actions. Focus on catching each other doing something right and not doing something wrong.

4. Demonstrate Trust Through Your Actions

Trust can take time to regain and re-establish. As the leader of the organization, you must take accountability for following through on your part of the agreed upon actions.

THE WHEN

"When" to start earning and maintaining your organization's trust? Without question, you should start the very first day that you accept a leadership role. A trusting workplace ensures that your team and coworkers can expend discretionary energy to serve the overall good of the organization and not on worrying about what will happen next.

If you are starting a new job or role as the organization's leader, you should have *"I must earn everyone's trust"* as a major goal and milestone in your "first ninety-day" plan.

If you unfortunately find yourself in the position of needing to "regain trust", start your efforts today. Being perceived as trustworthy will make your job less stressful and more enjoyable.

CHAPTER TEN

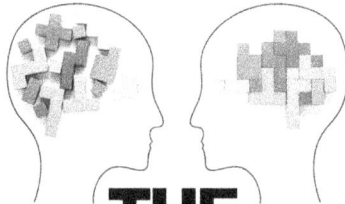

THE
SMART
LEADER
AND THE "SKINNY" PRINCIPLES

Ignorance is the Enemy of Good Decisions

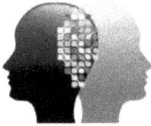

WHAT OTHERS ARE THINKING

"Inability to make decisions is one of the principal reasons executives fail. Deficiency in decision making ranks much higher than lack of specific knowledge or technical know-how as an indicator of leadership failure." — John C. Maxwell

John C. Maxwell

John Calvin Maxwell is an American author, speaker, and pastor who has written many books, primarily focusing on leadership. Titles include *"The 21 Irrefutable Laws of Leadership"* and *"The 21 Indispensable Qualities of a Leader"*. His books have sold millions of copies, with some on the New York Times Best Seller List.

A Situational Narrative

I SHOULD HAVE KNOWN

It's hard to believe that I started this adventure eight years ago. In some ways it feels like yesterday. Yet, in other ways it feels like an eternity.

At least when I wake up in the mornings these days, I don't have to be concerned with leading an $800M privately held company and 1,200 employees while managing a debt of over $350M. Maybe now, I can also sleep at night and perhaps spend more time enhancing my decision-making skills.

How did a thirty-seven-year-old woman with two engineering degrees, a Ph.D. in Robotics and a name like Julie Juliet get herself in this somewhat agonizing position?

Well, an idea I had as a young girl is the primary culprit. When I was about around fifteen, I remember my dear grandmother requiring the help of a patient care assistant. I vividly recall a situation where an assistant hurt her back twice lifting my dear grandmother out of bed. I felt so sorry for the healthcare worker. I knew she was committed to properly taking care of my Grammie.

I said to myself at that time, *"there has to be a way to perform these tasks in a gentle and respectful yet safer manner."* I also thought, *"I wonder if I could someday invent and sell a robot or something to help with this important job."*

After I graduated from a private university in California with my Doctoral Degree, I spent three years obtaining research grants. The grant funding allowed me to act upon and think technically about my idea. I worked solo on an initial design of a robotic system that could be used to help patient care assistants in their effort to support bedridden patients in hospitals and long-term care facilities. While visiting the new University Technology Incubator (UTI) that had just opened near my home, I met Joe, Jack and Johnny. They were leasing a small workplace in the UTI facility. I discovered that the three were working on several projects that utilized robotic controls. At first, they appeared to me to be standoffish and a little strange. However, as it turned out, they were just a group of entrepreneurial jocks with a couple of interesting patents.

After spending some time with them in their lab the next day, I realized that they were currently working on one project, which had technology like what I would need in my idea's design. The synergy between the guys and me was amazing. Within weeks, we had come to an agreement to focus, as a team, on the robotic system I was designing and, as the adage goes — the rest is history.

About a year later, Joe, Jack, Johnny and I formed a new startup company named Robotex. The following year, we won a contest sponsored by UTI and were awarded $1M of seed money to complete the development phase. Two years after that, we were able to raise our first round of venture capital funding. With those funds we were able to productionize a new robotic system we named "Robocare". By that time, we were all working in a manner like the "Mod Squad". We jokingly called ourselves the "4Jays". We were working full time and putting in twelve-hour days. We feverishly finalized testing, manufacturing specifications and the packaging of the proprietary firmware. The firmware was the embedded software written to control and interface with the patented touch & lift sensor technology.

To make a long story short, two years later, we secured a third round of venture capital funding. With the third round, we expanded product and training program sales to hundreds of healthcare facilities. To our surprise, within a couple of years, Robotex's annual gross revenue had increased to over $800M. Like most fast-growing technology startup companies, we were initially focused on capturing market share and not on profitability. With the rapid sales expansion, came significant production startup and marketing cost.

Consequently, part of my challenge at that point, as the now, President and CEO was to manage the heavy debt that Robotex was carrying on its balance sheet. I spent most of my time on the road convincing suppliers, investors and the financial markets that we had a vision of unlimited growth and would soon break even. It was also my primary responsibility to pave the way for the upcoming Robotex Initial Public Offering (IPO). Based on the estimated initial stock price of $45 a share, by going public via an IPO, we anticipated raising over $875M and paying off most of the company's growing debt.

This was the start of me discovering that, even though I had significantly developed my executive leadership skills in many areas, I was missing a vital executive skill — *sound decision-making*.
It wasn't until a month after we had selected an underwriter and began the "Due Diligence and Filings" step of the five-step IPO process that my poor decision-making skills began to reveal themselves. As a result, everything we had worked so hard for over the past eight years began to unravel.

The first requirment needed for the underwriting process was to develop the Robotex financial "Registration Statement". To ensure that the information provided in this key statement was accurate and without issues, the Robotex Board of Directors hired an independent investigation firm to review the backgrounds of all members of the Robotex senior management team. They were to also identify any legal problems faced by the company. To everyone's surprise, after the investigation, the underwriter determined that there were three major issues. All the issues would present significant risk for Robotex in its effort to move forward with the IPO. The issues dated back to the start of the company and all three centered around me not properly vetting the backgrounds of and my relationships with the other "Jays".

****

Here is a summation of the three issues:

1. When I made the decision to team with Joe, Jack and Johnny eight years ago, I didn't keep in mind the first step in any sound decision-making process — which is "gather information and verify the facts". As it turns out, Joe, now Robotex's Chief Financial Officer and the "face" to our investment partners, was convicted of financial fraud years ago. He had managed to successfully hide the conviction from everyone he now associates with. His deception included two legal name changes and multiple relocations.

   I was so impressed with the apparent synergy between us, that I didn't do the necessary due diligence on the backgrounds of my three new acquaintances and future business partners.

2. When I reviewed the robotic patents that Jack, now Robotex's Chief Technology Officer, had been awarded when he was a young engineer, I missed the fact that he was just one of eight engineers on the patent application. This would prevent Robotex from using the patents in our design unless the other seven engineers could be found, and a mutual agreement was signed.

   If I had known, I would have taken the second step in any sound decision-making process and would have identified all alternatives.

3. Johnny, now Robotex's Vice President and Director of Human Resources, had shared with me a few years ago that

an ex-employee, as a part of a sexual harassment complaint, was suing Robotex. At the time, I was deeply involved in some critical robotic testing. Therefore, I made the decision to allow Johnny to handle the work associated with obtaining a private settlement of the incident and have it sealed. I did get a briefing on the $325,000 that Robotex had to pay to settle the compliant.   However, I was never told that "Johnny" was the Robotex employee accused of the sexual harassment.

I was guilty of one of the most often-overlooked but important steps in the sound decision-making process — "thoughtfully reviewing all of your major decisions prior to pulling the trigger."

****

As I mentioned earlier, I am no longer with Robotex. Because of the findings of the independent investigator, the Robotex IPO was never completed. Six months after I was forced to resign as the President and CEO and to leave the company, a competitor who simply assumed the company's debt acquired Robotex. After I was released as President and CEO of the now defunct Robotex, I was asked to be the guest speaker at a local business development meeting. At first I was hesitant to do so. But later I decided to go ahead and accept their invitation and spoke to the group. I finally determined that at some point I must surface and share my experiences and lessons learned. I am glad that I did. Because in retrospect, though painful, the Robotex adventure turned out to be a meaningful professional and personal growth opportunity for me.

In making decisions in both my professional and personal life these days, I am extremely careful to not "short-circuit" the decision-making process. Never again do I want to be in the agonizing position of telling myself, *"I should have known"*.

WHAT OTHERS ARE THINKING

"When you see how the President makes political or policy decisions, you see who he is. The essence of the Presidency is decision-making." — Bob Woodward

Bob Woodward

Bob Woodward has worked for The Washington Post since 1971. He and Carl Bernstein are the authors of *"All the President's Men"* and *"The Final Days"*. Woodward has won nearly every American journalism award, and the Post won the 1973 Pulitzer Prize for his work with Bernstein on the Watergate scandal.

SKINNY PRINCIPLE #10

IGNORANCE IS THE ENEMY
OF GOOD DECISIONS

Ignorance in general terms refers to a lack of knowledge, understanding or information.

However, when it comes to the need to make good decisions within your organization, ignorance can be the difference between winning and losing. In a world full of uncertainty, not having the knowledge, understanding or information needed to make good, sound decisions creates a higher level of uncertainty.

Just as honesty, confidence, creativity and a positive attitude are considered a leader's "friends", when it comes to good decision-making — ignorance is a leader's "enemy".

Until a couple of decades ago, most organizations and their leaders had functioned in the murkiness of not having access to detailed and timely information and knowledge. Leaders made major decisions based on intuition and best available information about the past, present and future. The information age of the 21st century has created a new paradigm.

It is now possible for almost anyone to obtain near real-time knowledge and information with the click of a mouse. However, just as the current information-rich environment aids in instantly eliminating ignorance, it also can bring with it a new challenge — new levels of uncertainty, doubt and paralysis due to information overload.

The technological pervasiveness and complexity within most of today's organizations — both structural and interactively - have a tendency to create greater ambiguity and uncertainty. This includes making the challenge of predicting the future more difficult since every decade in the past thirty years bears less resemblance to the prior.

Combine these contemporary challenges with the fact that making effective, sound and quality decisions is an "art" that is learned through experience — the need for a well-matched, systematic decision-making process is an imperative.

A systematic decision-making process can help you and your organization make more deliberate, thoughtful decisions by organizing relevant information and defining alternatives. This approach increases the chance that your decision is the best alternative possible.

While most good managers and supervisors are aware of the need to possess and not "short-circuit" the decision-making process, many still find it difficult to overcome some common obstacles. These obstacles include the following.

- **Overconfidence** - Studies have shown that many managers and supervisors tend to overestimate their decision-making skills and abilities. This can lead them to making poor decisions by blocking out and not listening to any opposing opinions.

- **Confirmation Bias** - Confirmation bias occurs when leaders only pay attention to evidence or opinions that support their own. Thus, there is a tendency to not take into account important facts and hidden realities.

- **Anchoring Bias** - Anchoring bias occurs when leaders give too much weight to the first piece of information or the first idea that they hear. Thus, this information "anchors" their thinking. In this fixed position, they have a hard time changing their opinions when new information becomes available.

Recent research studies clearly demonstrate that there is a very high cost for poor decisions within organizational structures. As your organization's leader, enhancing your skills and abilities to make good, sound and quality decisions should be a life-long pursuit of excellence.

Here is the synopsis of "Skinny" Principle #10.

SKINNY PRINCIPLE #10

Ignorance is the Enemy of Good Decisions

This Principle draws attention to the fundamental truth that, as the leader of your organization, your ability to make good and sound decisions will determine your success or failure. Just as honesty, confidence, creativity and a positive attitude are considered a leader's "friends", when it comes to good decision-making — ignorance is a leader's "enemy". The decisions you make within your organization will not only influence the issues of the day. They will also affect your organization's future and they will, in many cases, cut across a wide range of social, cultural and political factors. As your organization's leader, it is your responsibility to establish and maintain a compatible and systematic decision-making process. The simplest way to think of what to keep in mind here is **"Because the strength of my decision-making skills and ability will always determine the magnitude of my organization's success or failure, I must keep my decision-making skills current and competitive."**

THE WHAT

The "What" here is that, as your organization's leader, you are the person vested with the responsibility to make good, sound and quality decisions. If you don't currently have a proven, systematic decision-making process and the ability to effectively deploy it, you should do what's necessary to fill the critical voids.

THE WHY

The "Why" here is based on the fact, that no organization, regardless of its type and size, can evade decision-making — and without exception, quality decision-making enhances the probability of organizational success.

THE HOW

As the leader of your organization, you encounter many decisions that need to be made every day. As your organization grows, the decisions you must make will increase in frequency and complexity. In addition, the decisions you make today can affect you and your organization far into the future. It may take years for the full effect of your decisions to surface.

As you will recall, it took over eight years for some crucial decisions made by Julie Juliet in this chapter's narrative to surface. By taking, the time and using a more thoughtful decision-making process to make what, at the time, appeared to be three straightforward decisions, Julie and Robotex could have landed in an entirely different space. It was the difference between her organization's success and failure.

When a decision must be made, here's "How" you can ensure that you consistently make the best decision available.

1. **Identify and Understand the Decision**

    This is an extremely important first step. You should take the time to understand the reasons why you "must" make a decision. Start this step by clearly defining the nature of the decision and weighting the consequences of "not" making a decision at this time.

2. Gather All of the Pertinent Information and Facts

You should gather all pertinent information before you enter into the final steps of the decision-making process. You should also perform an internal assessment as well as pursue information from external sources — including studies and market research. In some cases, you may need the support and advice of experts to gain a deeper understanding of your decision's potential effectiveness and the possible negative impact of the decision.

3. Identify All Available Alternatives

As you gather information, you should make a descriptive list of all available alternatives. You should always consider the opinions of others that you trust or get the advice of experts and professionals.

4. Compare and Evaluate Alternatives

You should evaluate each alternative in terms of feasibility, risk, impact and benefit as well as the potential positive and negative impact of the decision in the future.

5. Choose the Best Alternative

After you have considered the pros and cons, choose what you think and feel is the best alternative. However, prior to "pulling the trigger", you should walk away for a while and clear your mind. Then, return to make a final review of the decision. This will help to ensure that you have thoughtfully arrived at what should be the best decision available at the time.

6. Take Action

You should now take the action required to implement the alternative. This involves identifying what resources are required and gaining the required support of team members and all other stakeholders.

THE WHEN

"When" should you start using a proven, systematic decision-making process? We suggest that you start with your next major decision. By doing so, you will sleep better at night and feel confident that your decision was indeed the best decision you could have made.

THE SMART LEADER

"Management is doing things right. Leadership is doing the right things."
— *Peter Drucker*

Archetype Overview

S	**Studious Leaders** are learners in every aspect of life. Being studious as a leader allows you to see more than others see, see farther than the others see, and see things before the others see them. Studious Leaders take the time to honestly reflect on every response and every decision. Studious Leaders know that no other qualities emulate the impact of constant growth, life-long learning and the facing of one's fears.
M	**Masterful Leaders** stay true to their vision, practice humility and check their ego at the door. Passion and patience is a hallmark quality of Masterful Leaders. They nurture self-improvement themselves and in others. Masterful Leaders focus on activating the hearts of their people and making it a mission to support, encourage and create opportunities for their teams and others.
A	**Articulate Leaders** get everyone on the same page and never fail to communicate clearly and often. They ensure everyone knows the organization's overall goal through simple, concise communication. They know that keeping everyone moving in the same direction is critical to organizational success. Articulate Leaders extend their influence well beyond his or her department. Their effective communication skills exemplify and complement the executive presence required to lead.
R	**Resourceful Leaders** supplement others shortcomings, harness their team members' strengths and make themselves and those around them better. Resourceful Leaders learn to balance two important skills: *external sensing* and *internal conviction.* They are sharply sensitive to external cues from customers, associates and competitors. But they, concurrently, maintain the internal conviction required to push a visionary agenda forward, even when it's initially unpopular.
T	**Trustworthy Leaders** gain trust by always sharing the big picture and creating situational awareness. By creating awareness up and down the organizational chain of command they help to overcome the all-too-common culture of reactive responses, anti-change and cynicism. Trustworthy Leaders know that everything of value that we do in life revolves around relationships that are forged on trust.

WHAT OTHERS ARE THINKING

"Think simple — as my old master used to say - meaning reduce the whole of its parts into the simplest terms, getting back to first principles." —— Frank Lloyd Wright

Frank Lloyd Wright
Frank Lloyd Wright was an American architect, interior designer, writer, and educator, who designed more than 1,000 structures, 532 of which were completed. Wright believed in designing structures that were in harmony with humanity and its environment, a philosophy he called organic architecture.

THE "SKINNY" PRINCIPLES
Synopsis Table

SKINNY PRINCIPLE #1
It Does Matter

This Principle draws attention to the fundamental truth that your roles as the "Leader" and the "Manager" are two of the most critical roles within any organization. You can either strengthen or weaken the organization's chances for success. This Principle underscores the reality that while both roles are important, your role as the organization's "Leader" differs in approach, tone and expectations from your role as the organization's "Manager". Your ability to maintain the proper mindset, preparation and focus in each role can be the difference between winning and failing. The simplest way to think of what to keep in mind here is **"I should manage tasks, assets and deadlines and I should lead people, expectations and outcomes."**

SKINNY PRINCIPLE #2
What You Do Becomes Who You Are

This Principle draws attention to the fundamental truth that as the leader of your organization, "what you do", "when you do it" and the "results you achieve" are the major factors that determine "who you are" in the eyes, judgment and perception of your team and all others who matter. Also, "doing nothing" when action is required focuses an even brighter spotlight on a leader's lack of competency. The simplest way to think of what to keep in mind here is **"If I am asked to lead, I should always be authentic and do absolutely everything within my power to win. If I win, I am a winner with nothing to prove. If I fail, I am a failure with everything to prove."**

SKINNY PRINCIPLE #3
Where You Spend Your Time Is Not Your Choice

This Principle draws attention to the fundamental truth that as the leader of the organization, everyone wants and needs your time. Where you spend it, is "not your choice but your responsibility". It is your responsibility to make sure that your time is allocated wisely. Most effective leaders spend the majority of their time in three key areas: 1) Where they can prevent a pending crisis 2) Where, without their presence, a crisis cannot be resolved to the organization's best interest or 3) Where they sense a real need for encouragement, empathy or additional resources. The simplest way to think of what to keep in mind here is **"As a leader, I should spend the vast amount of my time where my presence can make an undeniable difference in achieving organizational goals. I should ask myself at the time, do I feel a little outside of my comfort zone here. If the answer is yes, then I know that — where I am — is where I should be."**

SKINNY PRINCIPLE #4
The Cards You Play Will Determine Who Wins

This Principle draws attention to the fundamental truth that, as the leader, your job is not to "do the work". Your job is to get the expected organizational results. As the organization's leader, it's your job and responsibility to understand the capabilities of each of the "cards" — aka team members — you are dealt [provided or selected] and to make sure that they are "all" in the best position to win and deliver the expected results. This job is somewhat like playing a game of Solitaire. In the real world, just as in Solitaire, you don't get to handpick all of your "playing cards". However, you must "read the hand you are dealt" and determine what it takes to win by placing each team member in the best position within the organization to contribute to the organization's goals. The simplest way to think of what to keep in mind here is **"As my organization's leader, my responsibility is to get the expected organizational results and not to do the work of others. My job is to ensure that each team member is in the best position to deliver what is needed and has the resources required to ensure an organizational victory."**

SKINNY PRINCIPLE #5
Being Present with Your Presence

This Principle draws attention to the fundamental truth that without you being "present with your presence", it is nearly impossible to develop organizational cohesiveness, gain concurrence among your work teams on strategy and create the organizational momentum required to win. As your organization's leader, you must ensure that performance challenges are adequately addressed at all three levels of leadership: *strategic, tactical* and *operational*. You should also remember that you are in the only position in your organization to globally "recognize," "organize" and "sell" the improvements and changes required. It is your responsibility to focus the proper attention and to be "present with your presence" at all levels. The simplest way to think of what to keep in mind here is **"I should always make sure that I am <u>present</u> and armed with my <u>presence</u> at all levels of organizational leadership."**

SKINNY PRINCIPLE #6
Empathy Can Pay Big Dividends

This Principle draws attention to the fundamental truth that being a skilled, competent and empathetic leader, allows you to reap significant dividends. Many of the dividends come in the form of both enhanced relationships with your team members and improved organizational performance. As an empathetic leader, you can better understand your team members as well as their skill sets, their aspirations and their needs. This can lead to enhanced team member contribution and professional growth. The simplest way to think of what to keep in mind here is **"I should remember that being empathetic with others in my organization is not the same as being sympathetic. When I am truly an empathetic leader, I feel what others are feeling. By doing so, I will come as close to reading their minds as humanly possible. Thus, I will gain hidden insights and place myself in the position to reap significant dividends for my organization and me."**

SKINNY PRINCIPLE #7

Success Happens When You Leave the Room

This Principle draws attention to the fundamental truth that it is not what team members think, say and do while you are present and in front of them. Your ultimate success will depend upon what happens when you leave the room. This Principle emphasizes the reality that when you perform your leadership role in a masterful way, your team members will perform up to and sometimes beyond the level of your expectations in your absence. As a masterful leader, you are expected to be knowledgeable. However, you are not expected to have all of the answers. You should be conscious and self-aware of what you know and acknowledge the need for your team members to fill in the blanks. The simplest way to think of what to keep in mind here is **"When I am a truly masterful leader, I can leave the room feeling that in my absence, all will be well. I should do this by being aware of what I personally bring to specific challenges while expanding the perspective and involvement of my team members to "do the work" required to win and to be successful."**

SKINNY PRINCIPLE #8

Winning the Battles Doesn't Always Win the War

This Principle draws attention to the fundamental truth that, as the leader, you have the responsibility for making sure that the battles your teams are winning are the battles that will lead to achieving your organization's overarching goals. If there is ever any doubt concerning how your team's goals, strategies and tactics stack up against those at the corporate level, you must have the wherewithal and courage to address the conflict head-on. Effective leaders know that it is their responsibility to recognize the conflict and to work at all levels of the organization. The simplest way to think of what to keep in mind here is **"I must remember that, as my organization's leader, my primary leadership focus should always be on the *forest* and not the *trees*"**.

SKINNY PRINCIPLE #9

Inspiring Mutual Trust is Job One

This Principle draws attention to the fundamental truth that as your organization's leader, you should make it a priority to develop and maintain the ability to establish, grow and re-build trust throughout your organization. Trust is an intellectual asset, a skill and an influencing power. However, trust is complex because it is intangible. Trust can be earned with competence, integrity, benevolence and credibility. Trust can be lost by being perceived as inauthentic, making false promises or lacking clarity in communications. When a team has trust in their leader, it improves communication, increases creativity and enhances productivity. The simplest way to think of what to keep in mind here is **"As a leader, I should never forget that it is the trustworthiness of my actions and behavior that matters most to my team and my organization."**

SKINNY PRINCIPLE #10
Ignorance is the Enemy of Good Decisions

This Principle draws attention to the fundamental truth that, as the leader of your organization, your ability to make good and sound decisions will determine your organization's success or failure. Just as honesty, confidence, creativity and a positive attitude are considered a leader's "friends", when it comes to good decision-making — ignorance is a leader's "enemy". The decisions you make within your organization will not only influence the issues of day. They will affect your organization's future and they will, in many cases, cut across a wide range of social, cultural and political factors. As your organization's leader, it is your responsibility to establish and maintain a compatible and systematic decision-making process. The simplest way to think of what to keep in mind here is **"Because the strength of my decision-making skills and ability will always determine the magnitude of my organization's success or failure, I must keep my decision-making skills current and competitive."**

WHAT OTHERS ARE THINKING

"Storytelling is the essential human activity. The harder the situation, the more essential it is" — Tim O'Brien

Tim O'Brien

William Timothy "Tim" O'Brien is an American novelist. He is best known for his book *"The Things They Carried"*, a collection of linked semi-autobiographical stories inspired by O'Brien's experiences in the Vietnam War. In 2010, the New York Times described O'Brien's book as a Vietnam classic.

The Narrative Storylines

CHAPTER 1: It Does Matter

NARRATIVE: No, My Dear. You Have A Leadership Dilemma

PROTAGONIST: Marilynn Mason-Lee, MBA, Manager (GS-14)
Federal Government Agency

STORYLINE: Marilynn is a senior and very successful manager working for a Federal Government Agency in the District of Columbia. Anticipating the opportunity to earn a job grade increase, she applies for a new leadership role within her Agency. Marilynn was not surprised that she was selected for the new position based on her years of management experience and her knowledge of internal operations. After a year of constant organizational turmoil, she now feels lonely, defeated and like a loser. During breakfast with an old friend and long-time mentor she shares her current office dilemma. To her surprise, Marilynn learns that the employee and organizational battles she's now facing seem to be mostly "self-inflicted" and related to her not understanding the difference between being a "Leader" and being a "Manager".

CHAPTER 2: What You Do Becomes Who You Are

NARRATIVE: I Thought They Really Knew Me

PROTAGONIST: Mark Ashford, MBA, PMP, Corporate Manager of Project Management

STORYLINE: Mark is one of forty-five managers attending a five-day Senior Leadership Development Program in San Diego offered by the Creative Leadership Academy. He was confident when he arrived that his leadership skills were well-known and respected by his superiors and the entire organization back home. He expected to enjoy watching the other attendee's faces drop in disbelief as they received the feedback from their 360-degree Leadership Assessments. However, Mark is surprised when his "letters from home" indicate that the leadership skills that helped him to be successful as a Senior Project Manager were insufficient for his new role as a Senior Functional Manager. His actions during the first months on the new job did not reflect those of the leader he thought he was.

CHAPTER 3: Where You Spend Your Time Is Not Your Choice

NARRATIVE: I Was Born To Do This

PROTAGONIST: CeCe Lane, PhD, Art Teacher, Small Business Owner

STORYLINE: CeCe grew up spending a lot of time with her Dad in the family custom furniture business. She loved the idea of reproducing antique furniture so much that she graduated from the University of Arizona with a PhD in Art History. After graduation, her Dad asked her to become a part of the store's leadership team and one-day run the family business. With great design skills and no confidence in herself as a leader and running a business, CeCe takes on the challenge to be an apprentice in her Dad's business. The goal is to find out if she has what it takes. Somewhat to her surprise, she easily learns some important lessons about overseeing a small business. She also receives some valuable advice from her Dad regarding how, as a leader, she should spend her time within the organization. This special piece of advice played a key role in her successfully taking over the family business and convincing herself that she does have what it takes.

CHAPTER 4: The Cards You Play Will Determine Who Wins

NARRATIVE: I Simply Played The Cards I Was Dealt

PROTAGONIST: Sara Hornbill, CEO, Walbash International, Multi-National Specialty Products Company

STORYLINE: Sara takes the unusual action to summon Alex Vanberry, one of her star General Managers, to travel from his store location in Lisbon to join her at the corporate office in New York City. She wants to gain a personal understanding of how he had accomplished an amazing turn-around by revamping a failing specialty products store location. It was a store that was on Sara's radar to close due to poor performance. Alex agreed to take on the new management challenge understanding that he could take only two of his current management team members with him to Portugal. Sara wanted to get the "skinny" on how the turn-around was accomplished. She also was very interested in determining if Alex's amazing feat could be replicated within other Walbash International locations in the European Union. After listening to Alex's thoughtful responses to a set of specific questions, Sara was not surprised that replicating the feat requires more than just being a good General Manager.

CHAPTER 5: Being Present With Your Presence

NARRATIVE: An Astonishing Lack Of Leadership Presence

PROTAGONIST: Anthony Jerome McAdoo, 30-year Corporate Retiree and Leadership Development Consultant

STORYLINE: Anthony recently retired as the Head of Data Center Management for the Capital Cargo Bank. While attending an Executive Leadership Conference in his new role as a Leadership Development Consultant, he surprisingly meets Ralph Dean, the new President of the Capital Cargo Bank. AJ — as he likes to be called — had dinner with Ralph that evening, As a result of their conversation; he left the conference with a new consulting engagement reporting directly to Ralph. He had a week to fly down to Capital Cargo's Charlotte Data Center and see if he could determine why the Bank had recently experienced multiple outages of their online banking systems. The problem had been traced back to the Charlotte Data Center. But, after multiple prior attempts, Ralph could not get an explanation that would "hold water" and was suitable to be presented to his Board of Directors during an upcoming meeting. What AJ found and reported back to Ralph a week later was not a real surprise. However, the degree of leadership "absence" in the Charlotte Data Center was astonishing.

CHAPTER 6: Empathy Pays Big Dividends

NARRATIVE: I Didn't Expect This

PROTAGONIST: Rebecca Bushman, MBA, Regional Vice President, Roland Pharmaceuticals

STORYLINE: Rebecca leaves her Sales Management position with a major wholesale distributor and joins Roland Pharmaceuticals. Roland was a new start-up company owned by Bob and Jennifer Roland. They were a nice, entrepreneurial-minded couple that Rebecca befriended while working on her MBA at Denver College. In short order, Rebecca became a Regional Vice President. She and three other Regional Vice Presidents were challenged with the need to achieve their assigned annual sales quotas to help ensure that Roland Pharmaceuticals was in the financial position to successfully execute its plan to go public via an IPO the following spring. As fate would have it, all three of Rebecca's top Sales Representatives are simultaneously beset with health, family and personal challenges. In the end, the question would become, "Could Rebecca generate and wrap the proper amount of empathy around this leadership dilemma and achieve her Region's sales commitment to Bob and Jennifer?"

CHAPTER 7: Success Happens When You Leave The Room

NARRATIVE: Now, It Makes Sense

PROTAGONIST: Candace Campbell, BA, MA, Chief of Police, City of Phoenix

STORYLINE: Candace's Mother was six feet tall. Her Father was six feet five. As an only child, Candace was gifted with her grandmother's height of only five feet four. However, today she finds herself sitting on a stage waiting to hear her name called and to take the oath to become the first female Chief of Police for a major U.S. Metropolitan area. In her response to the question, "how did you get here," she shares an insightful chronological breakdown of the "stops" along the way and the "leadership growth" that was required of her to pull it off. In the end, it was something that her Father told her years earlier – about being a leader – that was a major factor in her life's success and for her earning the opportunity to be selected as Phoenix's new Chief of Police.

CHAPTER 8: Winning The Battles Doesn't Always Win The War

NARRATIVE: The Trees Got Me

PROTAGONIST: Frances Rodriquez, Lead Supervisor, Miracle Mile Aerospace

STORYLINE: Frances finds herself sitting in her home office updating her resume. She had recently lost her job as a Lead Supervisor at Miracle Mile Aerospace. Six months earlier, she was on a roll doing what she thought was being asked of her as a responsible department leader. The successful implementation of the new SAMP initiative within her department would have most likely earned her a promotion and a much needed salary increase. However, today, as Frances painfully reflects upon how she landed in this dreadful situation, she now clearly sees "what she did" and "what she didn't do". She is now constantly reminded of a factor that is critical to the establishment of department-level "goals", "strategy" and "tactics" within any organization. It is a factor that should never be ignored. She is also reminded that the consequences of leaders "winning the wrong battles" internally can be devastating for themselves and their organizations.

CHAPTER 9: Trust Is Earned And Lost Prior To Becoming Visible

NARRATIVE: I Only Needed To Be Like Mike

PROTAGONIST: Charlie Yang, President and CEO, The Better Way Foundation

STORYLINE: About five years ago, The Better Way Foundation lost their President, CEO and Founder, Michael (Mike) Monahan, due to a long illness. Mike was viewed as a "trusted" leader and was respected by the entire organization. A year later, Charlie Yang joined the Better Way as only the second Chief Executive in the history of the twenty-five-year-old organization. After four years as the organization's leader, Charlie was viewed as the "second coming of Mike" and rewarded with a second, four-year employment agreement. Then, he decided to make some major changes to the Better Way's leadership approach and business strategy. The well-intended efforts resulted in Charlie losing the trust of the entire organization. A long-time member of the Better Way's Board of Directors, who was on the Board when Charlie was first hired, shares how it all started and what Charlie had to do to retain his job as the Better Way Foundation's President and CEO.

CHAPTER 10: Ignorance Is The Enemy Of Good Decisions

NARRATIVE: I Should Have Known

PROTAGONIST: Julie Juliet, MSEE, Ph.D., President and CEO, Robotex, Inc.

STORYLINE: An "idea" that Julie Juliet had, as a young girl, to help Patient Care Assistants perform their jobs in a safer manner is what drove Julie to earn a Ph.D. in Robotics. This focused drive and tenacity, eventually earned her the position of President and CEO of an $800M privately held company. Eight years after being one of the four founders of Robotex, she was charged with doing what was necessary to take the company public via an IPO. As a part of the process, the Robotex Board of Directors hired an independent investigator to perform a "due diligence" review of the company. The review included all aspects of the company's operations, including the background of Robotex's senior management team. Following the review, Julie began to discover that, even though she had significantly developed her executive leadership skills, she had missed a vital executive skill — sound decision-making. The independent investigation unveiled three poor decisions that Julie made over the previous eight years that would unfortunately torpedo the company's IPO and alter its future.

WHAT OTHERS ARE THINKING

"We give our time away all day long, to emotions that gain us no advantages, to people who do not value our time, to inefficient habits. If you want to take back this time, you need to cut to the chase." — Stuart R. Levine

Stuart R. Levine

Stuart Levine is chairman and CEO of Stuart Levine & Associates LLC, an international consulting and leadership training company that received PricewaterhouseCooper's 1999 Innovator of the Year award.

ABOUT THE AUTHORS

Charlotte D. Grant-Cobb, PhD

Charlotte is a gifted author, change management coach and professional mentor. She is a highly sort after International Coaching Federation (ICF) Certified Coach.

Charlotte's extensive resume includes over 30 years of professional accomplishment. She had held senior leadership positions within Fortune 100 corporations, small business enterprises as well as in Federal and State government.

Charlotte earned her Bachelor of Science degree in Management and a Master of Business Administration degree from *Arizona State University*. She has also earned a professional Doctor of Philosophy in Nutrition Counseling degree from *LaSalle University*.

Charlotte uses her gifts to inspire her clients to gain new awareness, create new habits, forge new pathways and embrace new experiences.

Ervin (Earl) Cobb

Earl is an accomplished corporate executive, leadership development coach, lecturer and entrepreneur. He is currently the CEO & Managing Partner of Richer Life, LLC.

Earl has held technical and leadership positions within Fortune 100, Mid-market and Venture companies including *Honeywell, Inc., Motorola, Inc., The Reynolds and Reynolds Company* and *Wells Fargo Bank*. He is the former President, COO and CEO of the high-tech start-up, *MedContrax, Inc.*

Earl earned a Bachelor of Science degree in Electrical Engineering, with honors, from *Tennessee State University*. He graduated from *Arizona State University* with a Master of Science degree in Engineering.

Earl is a former Adjunct Professor of Management at the Keller Graduate School of Management of *DeVry University*. He has completed graduate studies at *Stanford University's Graduate School of Business, the Sloan School of Management at MIT* and the *Center for Creative Leadership*.

OTHER BOOKS BY

Ervin (Earl) Cobb and Charlotte D. Grant-Cobb, PhD

Situations and Leadership
Short Stories and Lifelong Lessons

Leadership Front and Center
A Decade of Thought and Tutelage

Driving Ultimate Project Performance
Transforming from Project Manager to Project Leader

**The Official Leadership Checklist and Diary
for Project Management Professionals**

The Leadership Advantage
Do More. Lead More. Earn More.

God's Goodness & Our Mindfulness
Responding versus Reacting to Life Changing Circumstances

Focused Leadership
What You Can Do Today To Become a More Effective Leader

Transition
Solace and Comfort for the Broken Hearted

Pillow Talk Consciousness
Intimate Reflections on America's 100 Most Interesting
Thoughts and Suspicions

Navigating the Life Enrichment Model™

Living a Richer Life
Getting the Most out of Life's Gifts and Circumstances

Until I Change
Affirmations for Mastering Personal Change

www.ingramcontent.com/pod-product-compliance
Lightning Source LLC
Chambersburg PA
CBHW031328210326
41519CB00048B/3594